# Wild Flowers

## Martin Walters

HarperCollinsPublishers
77–85 Fulham Palace Road
London W6 8JB

www.collins.co.uk

First published 1994
Second edition published 2004
This edition published 2012

10 9

All pictures have been researched and supplied via Natural Image. Photographs are copyright Bob Gibbons apart from the following: Peter Brough 212; Andrew Gagg 79, 248; John Roberts 252; Peter Wilson 32, 46, 60, 87, 139, 152, 190, 191, 204, 241, 246 (right).

Illustrations from Collins New Generation Guide Wild Flowers of Britain and Northern Europe

The author asserts his moral right to be identified as the author of this work

A catalogue record for this book is available from the British Library.

ISBN 978-0-00-717854-4

Design by Liz Bourne
Printed in China by South China Printing Co. Ltd

Find out more about HarperCollins and the environment at
www.harpercollins.co.uk/green

# Contents key

The species in this book fall roughly into 21 different flower shapes. You should be able to match the flower shape of the species you are trying to identify to one of the drawings below, to find out to which family it belongs. Once you have looked up the right family section, you should be able to find your species. Some flower shapes are distinctive and characteristic of one family only. Others, e.g. regular flowers with 5 petals, appear in several families, and the key will direct you to all of these. The family name and a sketch of the flower shape appear at the top of each species entry page.

4

**Daisy Family** p.208, 211–213, 215, 219, 221–223, 230–239

**Carrot Family** p.106–120

**Bindweed Family** p.147–150

**Nightshade Family** p.153, 154
**Bellflower Family** p.189–192
**Lily Family** p.240, 242
**Daffodil Family** p.245

**Fumitory Family** p.27, 28
**Borage Family** p.142, 143
**Figwort Family** p.167, 169
**Honeysuckle Family** p.201

**Milkwort Family** p.47

**Pea Family** p.75, 81, 83–86

**Mint Family** p.176, 177, 179–184, 186, 188

**Violet Family** p.41–46
**Balsam Family** p.74
**Figwort Family** p.156, 157

**Heath Family** p.125–127

**Figwort Family** p.159–166, 170

**Arum Family** p. 252

**Spurge Family** p.122, 123

**Iris Family** p.246

**Daffodil Family** p.244

# Introduction

This book will help you identify the most common wildflowers of Britain and Ireland. There are about 1600 species of wildflower in these islands. The 288 in this book are those most likely to be seen during a walk in the countryside, be it on the coast or in the mountains, woodlands, hedgerows, fields or wetlands. **All those terms printed in bold in the species entries will be explained in this introduction.**

## WHAT IS A WILDFLOWER?

Wildflowers are those flowers which grow naturally in the countryside. Many are **native** – they form part of the original flora and have not been introduced by people. Others have been **introduced** either deliberately or via gardens (**garden escapes**) or farms. Many cultivated plants grown for food or medicine are descended from **ancestors** which still grow wild today (e.g. Wild Carrot, p.119). Some wildflowers are called 'weeds' simply when they grow where they are not wanted, usually in gardens or fields. They can be very pretty.

## THE FLOWER

A typical flower has a ring of **petals** which make up the **corolla**. Often brightly coloured, they give the flower its main colour. Some species have a tube-like extension or **spur** at the back of the flower. Below the petals is another ring or **calyx** of petal-like **sepals** which protect the flower when it is in bud. Although usually green or brown, some sepals are brightly coloured. Outside the sepals there may be special leaves or **bracts** which also protect the flower.

At the centre of a flower there is usually a tall column or **style**, topped by the sometimes feathery **stigma** – this is the

**Parts of a flower**

stamen [ anther
filament

petal

stigma

style

sepal

female part and is where the **pollen** (the male reproductive cells) from a male flower lands during pollination (the first stage in reproduction). The male parts are the **stamens** which each consist of a tall, thin stalk or **filament**, with an enlarged part called the **anther** at the top containing the pollen. Not all flowers are both male and female, some are single sex only.

A shoot may have a single flower at its tip, but more often there are several flowers arranged in a number of different ways. If the group of flowers is tightly packed, it may be called a **flowerhead**. Sometimes (see Daisy Family) the flowerhead may look like a single flower, but is actually made up of many tiny flowers or **florets** which which may look like the single petal of a normal flower. These petal-like florets are **ray florets**, those florets at the centre of the Daisy flower are **tube** or **disc florets**. A **spike** is a flowerhead in which all the flowers are attached to a single column. The flowers of the Carrot Family (**umbellifers**) grow in an arrangement known as an **umbel** – many flowers arise from the same point on the stalk, to form a flat-topped umbrella shape. In

Lords-and-ladies (p.252), each 'flower' is in fact the central rod (extended stem) or **spadix**, enclosed by a translucent hood or **spathe**. The actual flowers are tiny and grow at the base of the spadix.

## THE STEM

The **stem** is the main above-ground part of a plant, and normally grows upwards. There are many different kinds of stem. **Rhizomes** are underground stems. **Runners** grow horizontally above or below the ground and develop small roots and new plants at their tips. Some parts of the stem or leaf may develop **tendrils**, which aid climbing plants. **Bulbs** are undergound stems, with compressed, fleshy leaves, from which flowers such as Daffodils grow up quickly in the spring. **Bulbils** are like tiny bulbs which fall off the parent plant, and grow into new plants the next season. Some species, such as many thistles, have stems which are flattened at the edges (**winged** stems).

## THE LEAF

Leaves grow out from the sides of the plant, from thickened parts of the stem called **nodes**. They may grow **opposite** each other, or be **alternate** up the stem. When several leaves grow round the stem at each node, they are described as **whorled** or in **whorls**. Leaves growing at the bottom of the stem are called **base** or **basal** leaves. When these all spread from the centre they are known as a **rosette**. Those higher up are called **stem leaves**. The angle where the leaf stem joins the main stem is called the **axil**. **Bracts** are leaves growing close to a flower or flowerhead and protecting it. Sometimes leaf-like **stipules** grow at the base of a leafstalk.

A leaf consists of the leafstalk or **petiole**, and the **blade** which has a number of **veins**, including a central vein or **midrib**. **Simple** leaves have an undivided blade, while **compound** leaves are made up of separate **leaflets**. When these grow from the same point, like the fingers of a hand, the leaf is described as **palmate**. When they grow along either side, the leaf is **pinnate**.

Leaves can be a number of different shapes, including: **linear** (long and narrow), **lanceolate** (tapering like the blade of a lance), **oval**, **oblong**, **triangular**, **spoon-shaped**, **kidney-shaped**, **heart-shaped**, **trifoliate** (like a clover leaf), **spear-shaped**, **arrow-shaped**. Leaves may have smooth edges, or they may be **toothed** or **lobed**.

## THE FRUIT

The fruit develops in the flower after pollination, and protects the seeds until they are ripe. There are many different fruit types: some are fleshy and edible, and eaten by birds and other animals; others are hooked and cling to fur or clothing; and others are **pods** or **capsules** which release seeds when dry.

## DANGER AND CONSERVATION

Although culinary and medicinal uses of plants are given in this book, many species are **poisonous** (some, e.g. Hemlock, very poisonous), including many used in herbal medicine. **Do not eat any wild plant or prepare and use your own natural medicines. Do not pick or uproot any wild flower** – many are rare and specially protected. No wildflower may be uprooted without permission.

## HOW TO IDENTIFY WILDFLOWERS

If you know the name of a wildflower you can simply look it up in the **index** of common names at the back of the book. Closely related flowers belong to the same **family**. If you cannot identify a flower, but think it is related to one you do recognise, then look up the one you know and look through the species in its family (the family name appears at the top of each page). It is likely that your new find will be in that section. If you have no idea what your flower is, use the symbols in the **contents pages** (pp. 3–6) to decide what kind of flower shape it has. Then look through the families which contain flowers of that shape. The flower shape of each species appears at the top of each species entry page. Many families have a distinctive flower shape (e.g. the Bindweed Family). Others (e.g. the Daisy Family) contain species with different flower shapes, and thus have more than one characteristic shape.

## FLOWER NAMES

The **common (English) names** of flowers vary, but for most there is a recommended name which we have used. Well-known alternatives are also listed. Many names are very old and derived from traditional medicinal or culinary uses of the plant. Where these origins are known, we have given them. Every species also has a unique **scientific (Latin)** name, which is unvarying and international. It is always italicised and in two parts (binomial): the **genus** name is written first, with an initial capital letter, followed by the specific name eg *Viola lutea*. (Each **family** contains one or more genera (singular: genus), a genus being a group of similar **species**.)

## SPECIES ENTRIES

The first paragraph provides a general description of the plant (climber, shrub, etc.), with notes on the size, colour and shape of its leaves and flowers. For most flowers the width of the open flower is given (e.g. 8 mm across), but for long, narrower flowers, the length is given (e.g. 8 mm long). Flower colour on its own is not a good guide to identification – many species share colour, and it may vary within a species or with the season. Leaf shapes vary but they can aid identification, when combined with other features.

| | |
|---|---|
| **SIZE** | is the average height of the plant. Most grow upright, but some creep along the ground or climb on other plants, in which case the length of the spreading plant is given. |
| **HABITAT** | notes the main type of country where the species grows. Many are typically found in a particular habitat – e.g. marsh. This information may help confirm identification. |
| **RANGE** | gives the area in which the species might be found. Some, for example, only grow in warmer sites in the south, while others are restricted to mountains of the north and west. |
| **FLOWERS** | is when to see the species in flower. This aids identification, as similar species may have different flowering periods. |
| **SIMILAR SPECIES** | are those common species which might easily be confused with the main species described. |

Also known as Kingcup. A large buttercup with big, glossy, deep-green, kidney-shaped leaves. The bright yellow flowers look like giant buttercups and appear in spring and early summer. They are bigger than those of other buttercups, up to 5 cm across when fully opened. Clumps of Marsh Marigolds tend to hug the banks of streams. In late summer produces claw-shaped seed **pods**.

**SIZE** To 50 cm.

**HABITAT** Grows alongside ditches and streams. Also in marshes and wet woods.

**RANGE** Throughout Britain and Ireland, up to 1000 m.

**FLOWERS** March–July

# Wood Anemone

14 *Anemone nemorosa*

One of our prettiest early spring woodland flowers. Large patches of the woodland floor are sometimes carpeted with this species. It has star-like, 6-petalled white or pinkish flowers set against dark green, three-lobed leaves. The flowers are about 4 cm across.

**SIZE** To 30 cm.

**HABITAT** Mainly deciduous woodland. Also hedges and shaded banks.

**RANGE** Throughout, but very local in S Ireland.

**FLOWERS** March–May

Also known as Old Man's Beard because of its white feathery fruits. Climbs and twines up trees and in hedges. Develops small, creamy-coloured, fragrant flowers, about 2 cm across, which grow in clusters. The leaves usually have five leaflets. The downy fruits develop in September and October. Each fruit or **achene** has a feather-like **style** attached.

**SIZE** Stems to 30 m

**HABITAT** Mainly on calcareous soils, often in the shade of trees and thick hedges, and along the margins of woods.

**RANGE** Common, but only in southern England, south of the Mersey-Humber line, and in Wales.

**FLOWERS** July–August

# ✿ Meadow Buttercup

16 *Ranunculus acris*

Tallest of the three common buttercups (see also Creeping Buttercup p.17 and Bulbous Buttercup p.18). The **sepals** are cupped around the bright yellow flowers which are 18–25 mm across. Unlike those of the other two buttercups, the flower-stalks are not furrowed. The leaves are lobed and hairy.

**SIZE** To 1 m

**HABITAT** Damp meadows and pastures. Also found on rocks and ledges in mountains.

**RANGE** Common throughout

**FLOWERS** June–July

Creeps through grasses by means of long shoots or runners. Roots grow from these **runners** and form new plants which grow in large, often circular, patches. The flowers are 2–3 cm across. The **sepals** encircle the petals and the flower-stalks are furrowed. The leaves are lobed and hairy.

**SIZE** To 60 cm

**HABITAT** Damp and wet meadows and pastures. Also wet woods, sand dunes and roadsides. Survives mowing, and therefore common on lawns.

**RANGE** Common throughout

**FLOWERS** May–August

# Bulbous Buttercup

*Ranunculus bulbosus*

The common name refers to the swollen base of the stem. The plant is best identified by the **sepals**, which turn back from the flower, along the stems. The flowers are 2–3 cm across and the flower stalks are furrowed. The leaves are lobed and usually hairy.

**SIZE** To 45 cm

**HABITAT** Likes pastures, but avoids damp conditions. Prefers lime-rich soils.

**RANGE** Common throughout England and much of Wales; scattered in Scotland and Ireland.

**FLOWERS** May–June

Has bright yellow flowers, 2–3 cm across, each with 8–12 narrow petals and three **sepals**. Flowers fade with age to a creamy white colour. The leaves are rounded and glossy. An ointment for treating piles can be made from the fresh plant, so it is sometimes also called Pilewort.

**SIZE** To 25 cm

**HABITAT** Native woodland and grassland. Also grows alongside streams and as a garden weed.

**RANGE** Common throughout, but more scattered in S Ireland.

**FLOWERS** March–May

*Thalictrum flavum*

Tall plant with fluffy clusters (about 10 cm across) of tiny yellowish flowers. The yellow colour comes from the long **stamens** which are the most distinctive part of the flowers. The stems are rather firm and furrowed and the leaves divided. Could be confused with Meadowsweet (p.87) when seen from a distance.

**SIZE** To 1 m

**HABITAT** Wet meadows, marshes and fens. Also river banks.

**RANGE** Scattered in most of England except extreme SW; rarer in Wales and Ireland; virtually unknown in Scotland.

**FLOWERS** July–August

The largest and most showy of waterplants, with big, floating white flowers each with about 20 petals, and up to about 20 cm across. The floating leaves are round in outline, with a deep split almost to the centre, and there are no specialized underwater leaves.

**SIZE** Leaves are up to 30 cm across

**HABITAT** Lakes and ponds

**RANGE** Scattered throughout

**FLOWERS** July–August

# Yellow Water-lily

*Nuphar lutea*

22

Unlike White Water-lilies (p.21), these flowers stand up on stalks clear of the water surface. The yellow flowers are about 5 cm across and later develop into bottle-shaped fruit **capsules** (hence the alternative name 'Brandy-bottle'). The plant has oval-shaped floating leaves and lettuce-like underwater leaves.

**SIZE** Leaves are up to 30 cm long

**HABITAT** Lakes, ponds and slow streams

**RANGE** Scattered throughout, but commonest in S.

**FLOWERS** June–August

The commonest of our poppies, with large bright scarlet flowers, up to 10 cm across. Each flower has four rather crinkled petals, sometimes with a dark spot near the base. The leaves are deeply divided, with narrow segments. The fruit is a rounded 'pepper-pot' from which seeds are shaken by the wind.

**SIZE** To 60 cm

**HABITAT** A weed of cereal crops, especially along field margins which have escaped spraying with weedkillers. Sometimes grows in quantity along newly created road cuttings.

seed pod

**RANGE** Common throughout, but rarer in N and W.

**FLOWERS** June–August

# Long-headed Poppy

**POPPY FAMILY**

*Papaver dubium*

The flowers are sightly smaller, 3–7 cm across, and a paler red than Common Poppies (p.23). The leaves are divided, with shorter and broader segments than those of the Common Poppy. The fruit **capsule** is long, smooth and club-shaped.

**SIZE** To 60 cm

**HABITAT** Weed of arable fields and waste places

**RANGE** Throughout, including N and W where it is more common than the Common Poppy.

**FLOWERS** June–July

**seed pod**

A striking seaside species, this poppy has bright yellow flowers, and long, curved, horn-shaped fruit **pods**. The flowers are 6–9 cm across. Both leaves and stems are a soft blue-grey colour, and the leaves are deeply lobed.

**SIZE** To 80 cm

**HABITAT** Coastal shingle banks.

**RANGE** All around coasts, but mainly in S and W. N to Argyll and Berwick. Rather rare in Ireland.

**FLOWERS** June–September

# Greater Celandine

Badly named, as this is not related to the Lesser Celandine, but to the poppies. It has rather brittle stems and grey-green leaves, which exude a poisonous, bright orange sap when broken. The delicate flowers are bright yellow, 2–2.5 cm across and have four petals. The leaves are lobed, and each lobe has coarse teeth. Used in medicine to treat diseases of the gallbladder. Traditionally, the sap was applied to warts.

**SIZE** To 1 m

**HABITAT** Common alongside walls, banks and hedgerows. Most often found near houses, as an urban weed.

**RANGE** Throughout Britain, but rarer in Scotland; scattered in Ireland.

**FLOWERS** May–August

A pretty flower introduced from S Europe and escaped from gardens. Sprouts as clumps of pale green divided leaves from vertical walls in gardens or at the roadside. Each flowering stalk bears a group of up to 10 bright yellow flowers, 12–20 mm long, each with a short **spur**.

**SIZE** To 30 cm

**HABITAT** Old walls, growing from the mortar between bricks.

**RANGE** Common in England and Wales; local in Scotland and Ireland.

**FLOWERS** May–September

Our most common fumitory, this species
has feathery foliage and delicate clusters
of up to 20 pink and red flowers, each
7–9 mm long. Used in traditional
medicine to treat eczema.

**SIZE** To 40 cm

**HABITAT** A weed of cultivated land,
especially on light soils.

**RANGE** Especially E and central
Britain. Scarcer in the W and in Ireland.

**FLOWERS** May–October

# Charlock

*Sinapis arvensis*

Charlock has heads of bright yellow flowers, each 14–17 mm across. Its leaves are hairy and toothed or lobed. The upper leaves are stalkless and undivided. Its seed **pods** have straight tips, not curved as in the similar White Mustard (see below).

**SIZE** To 80 cm

**HABITAT** A common weed of cereal crops and field margins, especially on chalky or heavy soils. Much reduced by herbicides.

**RANGE** Throughout

**FLOWERS** May–July

**SIMILAR SPECIES**
White Mustard, *Sinapis alba* flowers
June–August and has more deeply lobed leaves.

Often obvious on grassy roadsides in late spring as patches of creamy-white **flowerheads**. The individual flowers are about 5 mm across, and their petals twice as long as their **sepals**. The leaves are oval and toothed. Fruits are heart-shaped seed **pods**.

**SIZE** To 1 m, but often smaller at roadsides.

**HABITAT** Introduced and now well established on roadsides and as an arable weed.

**RANGE** Commonest in S and E. Rarer in Scotland and Ireland.

**FLOWERS** May–June

# Field Penny-cress

Takes its name from its coin-shaped fruits which are flattened and almost circular, 12–20 mm across. The white flowers are very small (about 5 mm across). Smells unpleasant when crushed. The leaves are **lanceolate**.

**SIZE** To 60 cm

**HABITAT** A weed of waste ground and arable fields.

**RANGE** Much of England, but reduced by herbicides. Rarer in Wales, Scotland and Ireland.

**FLOWERS** May–July

# Shepherd's-purse

*Capsella bursa-pastoris*

This small weed is best identified by its heart-shaped fruits. These are nearly always present throughout the year, and give the plant its common name (they are shaped like the purses shepherds used to carry). The flowers are white and about 2.5 mm across. The base leaves are oblong in outline and grow as a **rosette** at ground level.

**SIZE** To 40 cm

**HABITAT** Weed of waste and cultivated ground.

**RANGE** Common throughout

**FLOWERS** January–December

The leaves are succulent, like those of many seaside plants, and heart-shaped. They are a source of Vitamin C and were used by sailors to prevent the disease known as scurvy. The plant is very variable in size. The flowers are about 8–10 mm across, with white (sometimes pink) petals. The fruits are rounded pea-shaped seed **pods**.

**SIZE** To 50 cm

**HABITAT** Coastal, on sea walls and banks, and in saltmarshes. Some forms also found inland, on mountain cliffs, streams and spoil-heaps.

**RANGE** All around coasts

**FLOWERS** May–August

*Cardamine pratensis*

Starts to flower about the same time as the
Cuckoo begins to call, hence the common
name. Also known as Milkmaids and Lady's
Smock. The flowers are pale lilac (sometimes
white), up to 2 cm across and have petals
about three times as long as the **sepals**.
The leaves are **pinnate**, like those of
watercress. Often flowers in large
patches in marshy areas.

**SIZE** To 60 cm

**HABITAT** Damp meadows,
pastures and along the banks
of streams

**RANGE** Common throughout

**FLOWERS** April–June

# Hairy Bitter-cress

Small plant with a **rosette** of leaves near to the ground. Flowers are white, about 4 mm across, and the petals are twice the length of the **sepals**. The leaves have rounded or oval leaflets. Bitter-cresses are edible and add a sharp flavour to salads.

**SIZE** 1 to 30 cm

**HABITAT** Garden weed, also found on bare ground such as scree slopes, walls and rocks.

**RANGE** Common throughout

**FLOWERS** April–August

**SIMILAR SPECIES** Wavy Bitter-cress, *Cardamine flexuosa*, is larger, with more zig-zag-shaped stems. Common in damp places. April–August.

# Winter-cress

*Barbarea vulgaris*

Winter-cress has small bright yellow flowers, 7–9 mm across, in fairly compact flowering heads. The lobed, shiny leaves can be used in salads. The stem-leaves clasp the stem at their base, and the uppermost stem-leaves are undivided.

**SIZE** To 1 m

**HABITAT** Roadsides, ditches, river banks, damp hedges.

**RANGE** Throughout lowlands, but less common in N.

**FLOWERS** May–August

# Garlic Mustard

*Alliaria petiolata*

Also commonly called Jack-by-the-hedge. Familiar
plant of hedgerows and also sometimes a garden
weed. Large heart-shaped leaves are characteristic
and smell like garlic when crushed. The flowering
heads consist of white flowers, each about 6 mm
across, with petals twice as long as **sepals**.

**SIZE** To 1.2 m

**HABITAT** Wood margins, hedgerows, shaded
gardens.

**RANGE** Throughout lowlands. Scattered in Ireland
and absent from much of N and W Scotland.

**FLOWERS** April–June

# Hedge Mustard

*Sisymbrium officinale*

A large, straggly weed with small yellow flowers, each only about 3 mm across. The branches are held stiffly out from the main stem and the fruits are thin **pods** that lie close to the branches. The base leaves are deeply lobed.

**SIZE** To 1 m

**HABITAT** Common weed of waste ground, roadsides, hedges and arable fields.

**RANGE** Throughout, but not in high hills and mountains.

**FLOWERS** June–July

A small plant with almost leafless stems rising from a **rosette** of spoon-shaped leaves at its base. The stem leaves are narrow and unstalked. The flowers are about 10 mm across with narrow pale yellow petals, about twice as long as the **sepals**.

**SIZE** To 50 cm

**HABITAT** Mainly on dry, especially sandy, soils, on walls, banks, and a garden weed.

**RANGE** Throughout, but scattered in W Scotland and in Ireland.

**FLOWERS** April–May

# Wild Mignonette

*Reseda lutea*

The deeply lobed leaves and narrow, rather compact yellow flower **spikes** make this species easy to identify. Each flower is about 6 mm across. Unlike the garden Mignonette, it is scentless.

**SIZE** To 75 cm

**HABITAT** Waste ground, arable field margins, especially on chalky soils.

**RANGE** Mainly in the E half of Britain. Scattered and more coastal in W and N, to about Argyll and Moray in Scotland. Introduced and rarer in Ireland.

**FLOWERS** June–August

**SIMILAR SPECIES** Weld, *Reseda luteola*, is a taller version, with narrow, unlobed leaves. June–August.

# Sweet Violet

*Viola odorata* 41

Has white or violet, sweet-smelling flowers, about 15 mm across. Puts out **runners** from which new plants grow. The leaves are long-stalked and heart-shaped at the base, with rather wavy edges. Used in herbal medicine to treat respiratory disorders.

**SIZE** To 10 cm tall

**HABITAT** Woodland, hedgerows, banks, railway cuttings, scrub, especially on chalky soils; often escapes from gardens.

**RANGE** England, Wales; rather local in Scotland and Ireland.

**FLOWERS** February–April

# Hairy Violet

*Viola hirta*

Rather like Sweet Violet (p.41), but its flowers are unscented and paler violet, and its leaves are more triangular and narrower. Each flower is 15 mm across. It has obvious hairs on its stems and leaf stalks.

**SIZE** To 5 cm

**HABITAT** Chalk grassland, scrub and open woods.

**RANGE** Mainly England and Wales; SE coastal Scotland. Rare in Ireland.

**FLOWERS** April–May

# Common Dog-violet

*Viola riviniana*

The most common wild violet, this plant
has leafy stems with heart-shaped leaves.
The flowers are 15–20 mm across, and
bluish-violet in colour with a pale **spur**.

**SIZE** To 15 cm, but very variable

**HABITAT** Woods and hedges, but also
pastures and mountain rocks

**RANGE** Common throughout

**FLOWERS** April–June

**SIMILAR SPECIES** Early Dog-violet, *Viola
reichenbachiana*, has a darker spur. S, E
and central England. March–May.

This plant has bluer flowers than the other dog-violets (p.43), each 15–25 mm across with a yellowish **spur**. The leaves are thick and narrowly triangular.

**SIZE** To 20 cm

**HABITAT** Rarer than other dog-violets. Heaths, dry grassland, dunes and fens. Not in woodland.

**RANGE** Scattered throughout

**FLOWERS** April–June

# Mountain Pansy

*Viola lutea* 45

The flowers are large (to about 3 cm) and either yellow, purple or a mixture of the two. The lower leaves are oval, the upper leaves **lanceolate**. All leaves are sparsely hairy, expecially on the veins and edges. The **stipules** are divided into 3–5 lobes. The plants have creeping **rhizomes**.

**SIZE** To 15 cm

**HABITAT** Grassland and rocky ledges in hilly areas, to about 1000 m.

**RANGE** Hills and mountains of Scotland, Wales and N England; very local in Ireland.

**FLOWERS** June–August

*Viola arvensis*

Has small creamy-white flowers, each with a yellow centre, and each about 15 mm in width. The **sepals** are pointed and often longer than the petals. The **stipules** are deeply lobed, with a large, toothed end-lobe.

**SIZE** About 15 cm

**HABITAT** Common weed of cultivated and waste ground, especially on neutral or chalky soils.

**RANGE** Throughout, but commoner in E half of Britain and SE Ireland.

**FLOWERS** April–October

**SIMILAR SPECIES** Wild Pansy, *Viola tricolor*, has larger yellow, white or purple flowers, April–September. Throughout, but less common in chalky areas of lowland England.

Rather variable in size and in flower colour.
The flowers (each up to 8 mm) resemble
those of the Pea Family (pp. 75–86) and are
blue, pink or white. The stems are thin and
feeble, with narrow, alternate leaves.

**SIZE** To 30 cm

**HABITAT** Grassland, heaths and dunes

**RANGE** Throughout

**FLOWERS** May–September

**SIMILAR SPECIES** Heath Milkwort, *Polygala
serpyllifolia*, more slender stems, opposite leaves
and bright blue flowers, May–August. Throughout.

*Hypericum perforatum*

One of the most common of our several St John's Worts. Has upright flowering stems, with opposite pairs of oval stalkless leaves covered in translucent spots. The flowers are yellow, 5-petalled and about 2 cm across. Used in the Middle Ages to treat wounds. The oil has anti-bacterial properties, and soothes burns.

**SIZE** To 1 m

**HABITAT** Open woods, hedgerows, waste ground, and grassland.

**RANGE** Throughout, but rare in central and W Scotland.

**FLOWERS** June–September

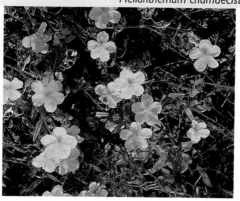

Creeping plant with woody stems and bright yellow flowers (about 2 cm across) with 5 petals. Rather weak, slender stems with narrow, opposite leaves. The leaves are whitish below and tend to curl over at the edges.

**SIZE** To 30 cm (often smaller).

**HABITAT** Chalky grassland and scrub.

**RANGE** Throughout most of Britain; very rare in Ireland, only in one locality in Co. Donegal.

**FLOWERS** June–September

# ✿ Bladder Campion

PINK
FAMILY

50 *Silene vulgaris*

This species is very closely related to the Sea Campion (p.51). It has white flowers and a bladder-like **calyx** behind the petals. The flowers are about 18 mm across. The leaves are oval and pointed, with wavy edges.

**SIZE** To 1 m

**HABITAT** Grows on waste ground and in hedgerows and banks.

**RANGE** Throughout most of Britain, though rarer in N and W. Scattered in Ireland, mainly central.

**FLOWERS** June–August

# Sea Campion

*Silene maritima*

Very like Bladder Campion (p.50) but has smaller, fleshy leaves,
larger flowers and a lower growth habit. Like Bladder
Campion, this species has a bladder-like **calyx**. The
flowers are 2–2.5 cm across.

**SIZE** Low cushions or mats, to about 25 cm high.

**HABITAT** Shingle and cliffs, mostly by the sea.

**RANGE** Throughout, almost always at the coast.

**FLOWERS** June–August

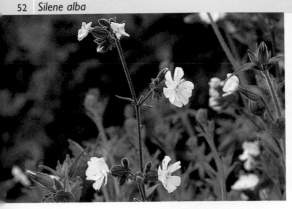

An attractive plant, whose large white flowers (to 3 cm across) remain fully open into the evening, and attract moths as pollinators. Male and female flowers grow on different plants. The leaves are oval or **lanceolate**. Unlike Bladder Campion (p.50) and Sea Campion (p.51) it does not have a bladder-like **calyx**.

**SIZE** To 1 m

**HABITAT**
Waste ground, rough field margins, hedgerows.

**RANGE** Common in most of lowland Britain. Rare in Ireland, Wales, SW England and highland Scotland.

**FLOWERS** May–September

# Red Campion

*Silene dioica* 53

A very decorative early summer flower, with large (to 2.5 cm across) red or deep pink flowers. Slightly smaller plant than White Campion (p.52), with rather smaller flowers. Flowers open in the day to attract bees and butterflies. Where it grows close to White Campion, hybrids with pink flowers are sometimes found. The leaves are oval or oblong. There are separate male and female plants.

**SIZE** To 80 cm

**HABITAT** More of a woodland edge flower (even under partial shade of trees) than White Campion. Also hedgerows and roadsides, especially near woods.

**RANGE** Common in much of Britain, but rarer in Ireland, W Scotland and also parts of E England.

**FLOWERS** May–July

# Ragged Robin

54 *Lychnis flos-cuculi*

The large flowers are rose-pink (occasionally white) and each of the five petals is deeply divided into four, giving this flower a ragged, almost scruffy, appearance. Each flower is 2.5 cm across. The leaves are narrow and lanceolate, and rough to the touch.

**SIZE** To 80 cm

**HABITAT** Wet meadows, fens and marshes, also wet woodland. Reduced by drainage and fertilization of lowland grassland.

**RANGE** Throughout

**FLOWERS** May–June

Rather large white flowers (to about 2 cm across) on thin, hairy stalks. The five white petals are deeply notched and longer than the **sepals**. The leaves are narrow and slightly hairy, giving this **genus** its common name.

**SIZE** To 20 cm

**HABITAT** Dry banks, dry grassland, especially in sandy or slightly acid soils.

**RANGE** Mainly in E. Rare in W and SW.

**FLOWERS** April–August

# ✿ Common Mouse-ear

*Cerastium fontanum*

Very common weed with rather trailing, hairy stems. Grouped white flowers are rather small (8–15 mm across, but very variable) with five notched petals, about the same length or slightly longer than the **sepals**. The leaves are narrow and hairy, hence its common name.

**SIZE** To 40 cm

**HABITAT** Grassland, shingle, tracks, sand dunes, cultivated and waste ground.

**RANGE** Common throughout

**FLOWERS** April–September

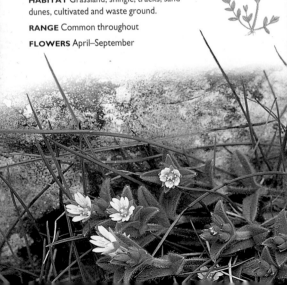

# Greater Stitchwort

*Stellaria holostea* 57

One of our prettiest woodland and hedgerow spring flowers. The white flowers, up to 3 cm across, grow on slender stalks. The petals are notched and longer than the green sepals. The leaves are narrow and stiff.

**SIZE** To 60 cm

**HABITAT** Hedges, banks and wood margins.

**RANGE** Common throughout most of Britain and Ireland, but rarer or absent in extreme N and W.

**FLOWERS** April–June

# Lesser Stitchwort

**PINK FAMILY**

*Stellaria graminea*

A more delicate plant than Greater Stitchwort (p.57), with smaller flowers and narrower leaves. The flowers are white and up to 10 mm across. The petals are deeply notched, and only just longer than the green **sepals**.

**SIZE** To 60 cm

**HABITAT** Dry, heathy ground.

**RANGE** Common throughout most of Britain and Ireland.

**FLOWERS** May–August

One of our most common weeds, it has very straggly growth and weak, juicy stems. Its white flowers are small, 5–10 mm across, with petals shorter than the green **sepals**. Often given to budgerigars and other cage birds. The leaves can be eaten in salads. Used as herbal medicine for skin diseases.

**SIZE** To 30cm, but very variable.

**HABITAT** Mostly on cultivated ground, especially as a weed in vegetable gardens. Also at edges of pastures, and on waste ground.

**RANGE** Common throughout

**FLOWERS** January–December

A small plant with broad, fleshy leaves. The stems grow close together, forming tight clumps in the dunes, or between pebbles on shingle beaches. The flowers are yellowish white and up to 10 mm across. The petals are about the same length or shorter than the **sepals**. The fruits are large, green and pea-like.

**SIZE** To 5 cm

**HABITAT** Dunes and shingle, near the sea.

**RANGE** Common on all coasts.

**FLOWERS** May–August

# Thyme-leaved Sandwort

*Arenaria serpyllifolia*

A small, common weed with inconspicuous white flowers, up to 8 mm across, in branched **flowerheads**. The petals are often shorter than the green **sepals**. The fruits are flask-shaped. Its leaves are small, about 6 mm long, and look like Thyme leaves, and its stems are hairy.

**SIZE** To 20 cm

**HABITAT** Bare, waste ground, either chalky or sandy, quarries, cliffs, dunes. Also grows on the tops of walls.

**RANGE** Throughout most of British Isles. Scattered in most of W Scotland and Ireland.

**FLOWERS** April–November

# Corn Spurrey

*Spergula arvensis*

A grey-green, straggly plant covered in sticky hairs. Long, narrow leaves grow in circular clusters (**whorls**) up the stems. The flowers are white, with five petals which are slightly longer than the **sepals**, and about 5 mm across. The fruits are **capsules** which turn downwards and split into five when ripe, releasing blackish seeds.

**SIZE** To 50 cm

**HABITAT** A weed of light, sandy soils, often in cornfields. Much reduced by herbicides.

**RANGE** Throughout

**FLOWERS** June–August

A pretty white or pale pink seaside flower. Each flower is up to 12 mm across, its five petals longer than its **sepals**. The leaves are fleshy. It produces a fruit **capsule** of about 10 mm in length, which contains large, flattened seeds.

**SIZE** To 30 cm

**HABITAT** Saltmarshes

**RANGE** Throughout, but not as widespread as Lesser Sea-spurrey (see below).

**FLOWERS** June–September

**SIMILAR SPECIES** Lesser Sea-spurrey, *Spergularia marina*; smaller pink flowers, petals shorter than sepals. Prefers drier parts of saltmarshes and inland salty soils. June–August.

# Springbeauty

*Montia perfoliata*

Unmistakable, with its small white flowers
set against two shiny leaves which are
completely joined around the stem. The
flowers are about 2 mm across.

**SIZE** To 30 cm

**HABITAT** Waste and cultivated ground,
especially on sandy soils. Also on dunes.

**RANGE** Introduced from N America. Mainly
in eastern part of Britain. Rare in Ireland.

**FLOWERS** May–July

A very attractive common flower, with large (to 4 cm across) pink flowers. Each of the five petals is marked with dark stripes. The leaves, which are large with rounded lobes, can be eaten in salads.

**SIZE** To 1 m

**HABITAT** Waste ground, roadsides.

**RANGE** Common in England; scattered in Wales, Scotland and Ireland.

**FLOWERS** June–September

**SIMILAR SPECIES** Dwarf Mallow, *Malva neglecta*, is low, with smaller, paler flowers, mainly S and E England. June–September.

*Lavatera arborea*

Looks like a giant, hairy version of the Common Mallow (p.65). This magnificent bushy plant has tall **spikes** of large pink-purple flowers, each 3–5 cm across. The roundish, velvety leaves are up to 20 cm across. The tall stems can be quite woody, hence the name 'Tree' Mallow. Makes a fine garden plant.

**SIZE** To 3 m

**HABITAT** Rocks and waste ground near the sea.

**RANGE** S and W coasts

**FLOWERS** July–September

The tall, grey stems and leaves are softly hairy. The leaves are sharply toothed and sometimes folded like a fan. The flowers are a delicate shade of palest pink, and up to 5 cm across. Extracts of Marsh Mallow are used to treat inflammation and ulcers. Also the source of the original marshmallow sweets.

**SIZE** To 1.2 m

**HABITAT** Brackish ditches and banks near the sea, and at upper (landward) end of saltmarshes.

**RANGE** Coasts of S Wales, S and E England and S and W Ireland.

**FLOWERS** August–September

A delicate, inconspicuous plant with small (4–6 mm across), white, five-petalled flowers, held up on thin, wiry stems. Although common, easily overlooked. The leaves are oblong and grow in opposite pairs.

**SIZE** To 25 cm

**HABITAT** Grassland, heaths, moorland, dunes, rock ledges.

**RANGE** Throughout

**FLOWERS** June–September

**SIMILAR SPECIES** Cultivated Flax, *Linum usitatissimum*, is commonly grown as a crop (linen and linseed oil), especially in E England. The flowers turn entire fields a bright pale blue in summer.

A common wild flower with deeply lobed, hairy leaves and hairy stems. The flowers are bright pink-purple (sometimes white) and up to 10 mm across. Like all cranesbills, the fruit has the long beak which gives this group its name, but in this species the fruit is hairless.

**SIZE** To 40 cm

**HABITAT** Dry grassland, waste land, dunes

**RANGE** Common throughout

**FLOWERS** April–September

**SIMILAR SPECIES** Small-flowered Cranesbill, *Geranium pusillum*, pale lilac flowers, 6 mm across, June–September, and hairy fruits. Common in England.

A pretty species with five-lobed leaves and thin, spreading, reddish stems. The flowers are 12–16 mm across and have five pink petals, with rounded ends. The **sepals** are red.

**SIZE** To 50 cm

**HABITAT** Woods, hedges, banks, rocks, shingle, and as an attractive weed in gardens.

**RANGE** Common throughout, but rarer in parts of N and NW. Scotland

**FLOWERS** May–September

Has large violet-blue flowers, each up to 4 cm across, with rounded petals, on long flower stalks. The leaves are rather feathery, being deeply cut, and have 5–7 lobes. Often grows in patches.

**SIZE** To 1 m

**HABITAT** Meadows and roadsides

**RANGE** Widespread in England and S Scotland. Rare in Ireland and local in Wales and N and W Scotland.

**FLOWERS** June–September

**SIMILAR SPECIES** Wood Cranesbill, *Geranium sylvaticum*, smaller, reddish-violet flowers, June–July, central and S Scotland and N England.

*Erodium cicutarium*

The flowers are a bright pink-purple (sometimes white) and about 7–16 mm across. The feathery leaves often grow as a **rosette** at the base of the plant. In storksbills the fruit is very long (in this case about 4 cm) and beak-shaped.

**SIZE** To 60 cm

**HABITAT** Dry grassland, arable fields on light soils and dunes.

**RANGE** Common around all coasts. Scattered inland in England.

**FLOWERS** June–September

Shamrock-like leaves identify this plant of the woodland floor. The large flowers are white, with five delicate petals veined in lilac, and up to 15 mm across.

**SIZE** To 15 cm

**HABITAT** Woods, hedges, shady rocks, mainly on acid soils.

**RANGE** Throughout, but rare in chalk and fenland areas of E Anglia.

**FLOWERS** April–May

# Indian Balsam

*Impatiens glandulifera*

Also called Policeman's Helmet. Introduced from Himalaya, it is a tall, hollow-stemmed plant with large opposite leaves and big purple-pink flowers, to about 4 cm long, with **spurs**. The fruits are oval **capsules** which explode when ripe and dry, releasing the seeds.

**SIZE** To 2 m

**HABITAT** River banks and wet waste places. Often by polluted streams in industrial areas.

**RANGE** Scattered throughout, except N and W Scotland. Most common in N England.

**FLOWERS** July–October

**SIMILAR SPECIES** Touch-me-not Balsam, *Impatiens noli-tangere*, smaller, with yellow, brown-spotted flowers.

Large, pink flowers (to 2 cm) characterize this restharrow, a pretty species with hairy stems. The leaves are usually made up of three toothed leaflets, but sometimes of only one leaflet. Spreads by sending out **rhizomes** which used to get caught in ploughs and harrows, hence its name.

**SIZE** To 40 cm

**HABITAT** Rough grassland, mainly on chalky soils, sand dunes

**RANGE** Common, but rare in N and W, where mainly coastal.

**FLOWERS** June–September

**SIMILAR SPECIES** Spiny Restharrow, *Ononis spinosa*, taller, with spines. England, not SW. June–September.

# Black Medick

**PEA FAMILY**

*Medicago lupulina*

This plant has small clusters of tiny (3 mm) yellow flowers, which later turn into black kidney-shaped **pods** in late summer and autumn. The leaves are a typical three-lobed cloverleaf, but the tip of each is extended into a minute point.

**SIZE** To 50 cm

**HABITAT** Grassland, roadsides

**RANGE** Widespread, except in N and NW of both Ireland and Scotland.

**FLOWERS** April–August

**SIMILAR SPECIES** Spotted Medick, *Medicago arabica*, has a black spot on each leaflet; mainly S and E England, and S Wales, April–August.

A tall species, with spikes of small (5–7 mm long), yellow flowers. The leaves each have three leaflets. The leaflets are about 15–30 mm long, oblong and toothed. The ripe fruits are hairy, black oval **pods**.

**SIZE** To 1.5 m

**HABITAT** Fields, roadsides and waste places

**RANGE** Lowland England, especially S and E. Rare and usually coastal elsewhere.

**FLOWERS** June–August

**SIMILAR SPECIES** Ribbed (Common) Melilot, *Melilotus officinalis*, has small yellow flowers (4–7 mm long) and hairless brown seed pods. Lowland England, rare elsewhere. June–September.

*Trifolium pratense*

The leaves are large typical cloverleaves with three leaflets. In Red Clover these often have pale white semicircular markings. The **flowerheads** are rounded and pink and up to 4 cm long. Used in herbal medicine to treat respiratory and skin disorders.

**SIZE** To 60 cm

**HABITAT** Grassy banks, roadsides, meadows

**RANGE** Throughout

**FLOWERS** May–September

**SIMILAR SPECIES** Zigzag Clover, *Trifolium medium*, has long, narrow leaflets; grassy banks and meadows; local, but rare in Ireland and N Scotland.

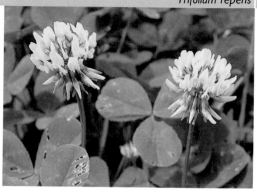

Commonest of the clovers, found in most types of grassland. The leaves are typical cloverleaf shape, with three leaflets. Like Red Clover (p.78), the leaflets normally have a pale band, but are sometimes heart-shaped. The flowers are white and clustered in heads of up to about 2 cm across.

**SIZE** To 50 cm

**HABITAT** Grassy banks, grassland, lawns

**RANGE** Throughout

**FLOWERS** June–September

# Kidney Vetch

*Anthyllis vulneraria*

This species has large, rather tightly packed heads of yellow, cream or red flowers at the top of a long stalk. The **flowerheads** are in pairs, each to about 4 cm across. After flowering, the heads become downy (the **calyces** are woolly). The leaves are hairy and made up of nine leaflets.

**SIZE** To 60 cm

**HABITAT** Dry, usually chalky soils, often coastal, frequently in grassland on cliff-tops.

**RANGE** Widespread throughout

**FLOWERS** June–September

# Bird's-foot Trefoil

*Lotus corniculatus* 81

A common, nearly hairless plant with large, bright yellow flowers.
The **flowerheads** are made up of about six flowers, each up to
about 15 mm long and sometimes streaked with red. The leaves
have three main leaflets, and there is also a pair of
smaller leaflets at base of the leaf-stalk.

**SIZE** To 40 cm

**HABITAT** Grassland

**RANGE** Throughout

**FLOWERS** June–September

**SIMILAR SPECIES**
Greater Bird's-foot Trefoil, *Lotus uliginosus*, 60 cm,
has a hollow stem, and heads of 8+ flowers,
June–August. Damp habitats throughout, but rare in central Ireland
and N and NW Scotland.

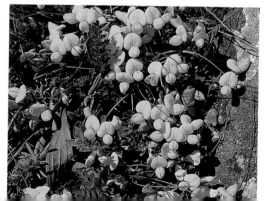

# Sainfoin

*Onobrychis viciifolia*

A beautiful plant with tall **spikes** of pink flowers (each flower about 15 mm long) on long stems. It has pretty leaves with 6–12 pairs of leaflets. Often escaped from cultivation (it is used as a forage crop for livestock), but a native form also exists. The name comes from the French and means healthy hay – a reference to its use as animal fodder.

**SIZE** To 60 cm

**HABITAT** Chalk and limestone grassland

**RANGE** Mainly S and E England (to S Yorkshire)

**FLOWERS** June–August

A fine climbing plant, with long **spikes** of blue or purple flowers, each flower to 12 mm long. There are up to 40 flowers in each spike. The leaves are made up of many paired leaflets and each leaf ends in a branched **tendril**.

**SIZE** To 2 m

**HABITAT** Hedges, rough grassland, meadows

**RANGE** Throughout, except highlands

**FLOWERS** June–August

# Bush Vetch

*Vicia sepium*

A climbing plant with short **spikes** of pale blue or purple flowers, each flower 12–15 mm long. The leaves, each made up of 2–3 pairs of leaflets, end in a branched **tendril**. Unlike the slightly hairy Common Vetch (p.85), this plant is almost hairless.

**SIZE** To 1 m

**HABITAT** Hedges, woodland edges and rough grassland

**RANGE** Throughout, except highlands

**FLOWERS** May–August

**SIMILAR SPECIES** Wood Vetch, *Vicia sylvatica*, has slightly larger flowers, white with purple or blue veins, in spikes of 5–15; woods, rocky sites, shingle and coastal cliffs; rather rare and local.

**SIZE** To 1.2 m

**HABITAT** Grassy areas, roadsides, waste places

**RANGE** Throughout lowlands, scattered in Ireland

**FLOWERS** May–September

The flowers of the Common Vetch are purple and usually single or in pairs. Each flower is 10–18 mm long. The leaves are made up of 3–8 pairs of leaflets. This plant is slightly hairy, unlike the almost hairless Bush Vetch (p.84).

# Meadow Vetchling

**PEA FAMILY**

*Lathyrus pratensis*

A common plant, with pale yellow flowers in clusters of up to 10. Each flower is 15–18 mm long. It has leaves made up of one or two pairs of leaflets, and branched **tendrils** with which it clambers up grass stems and other plants.

**SIZE** To 1.2 m

**HABITAT** Hedges, long grass

**RANGE** Common throughout, except Scottish Highlands

**FLOWERS** May–August

# Meadowsweet

*Filipendula ulmaria*

One of the prettiest wild flowers of marshy habitats. The small, creamy-white flowers, each about 4–8 mm across, are arranged in rather untidy clusters. The leaves have 2–5 pairs of leaflets and, when crushed, give off a distinctive, rather antiseptic smell. Once used to flavour mead, hence the name. This is the plant which first gave us aspirin, and it is still used as a herbal remedy for fevers, and for treating diarrhoea.

**SIZE** To 1.2 m

**HABITAT** Marshes, fens, river banks, damp meadows and other wet places.

**RANGE** Throughout

**FLOWERS** June–September

# Silverweed

88 *Potentilla anserina*

Best recognized by the silvery-backed **compound** leaves, with leaflets arranged in pairs. It has large yellow flowers (to about 2 cm across), with five petals. Frequently forms large patches over damp disturbed or trampled ground.

**SIZE** To 15 cm

**HABITAT** Dunes, wet pastures, roadsides, margins of ponds

**RANGE** Throughout, except Scottish Highlands

**FLOWERS** June–August

Tormentil has yellow flowers, about 10–15 mm
across, each with four petals. The leaves are a shiny
green, and most are made up of three rather
narrow leaflets. The plant has a tough, woody
base from which the stems and flowers grow up
each year. Used in herbal medicine to treat
diarrhoea and sore throats.

**SIZE** To 30 cm

**HABITAT** Heathy grassland, bogs, fens,
mountains, mostly on acid soils.

**RANGE** Throughout

**FLOWERS** June–September

# Creeping Cinquefoil

*Potentilla reptans*

Spreads by sending out long, creeping **runners** which root at intervals. The flowers are large (to 2.5 cm across) and yellow, with five petals. The **compound** leaves are made up of five (occasionally seven) narrow leaflets, which fan out from a central point. The name cinquefoil comes from the French word cinque meaning 'five'.

**SIZE** To 20 cm

**HABITAT** Hedges, banks, roadsides, grassland, waste places, mainly on neutral or alkaline soils.

**RANGE** Throughout, but rare in central and N Scotland, and scattered in N Ireland.

**FLOWERS** June–September

# Barren Strawberry

*Potentilla sterilis*

This is one of the earliest of our woodland species to come into flower. The Barren Strawberry looks very like the true Wild Strawberry (p.92), but it lacks the silky hairs under the leaves. The flowers are white and about 10–15 mm across, with gaps between the petals. It does not have the fleshy, edible fruits of Wild Strawberry, hence its common name.

**SIZE** To 15 cm

**HABITAT** Open woodland, woodland edges and scrub

**RANGE** Throughout, but rarer in N Scotland

**FLOWERS** February–May

Distinguished from the Barren Strawberry (p.91) by the silky hairs under its leaves, its larger petals and by its fruits. The flowers are white, about 12–18 mm across, with touching or slightly overlapping petals. The fruits are small, but delicious, red strawberries. Like the cultivated Garden Strawberry, *Fragaria* x *ananassa*, it spreads by rooting from **runners**.

**SIZE** To 30 cm

**HABITAT** Woods, clearings and scrub, especially on lime-rich soils.

**RANGE** Throughout, but rarer in N Scotland

**FLOWERS** April–July

Also known as Herb Bennet, from the old Latin *Herba benedicta*, 'blessed herb'. A straggly plant with tall, hairy stems, and toothed stem leaves. The yellow flowers look a bit like cinquefoils (p.90), but are small (8–15 mm across) and inconspicuous. They turn into tight, slightly prickly fruit heads. Used to treat piles and digestive disorders.

**SIZE** To 60 cm

**HABITAT** Scrub, hedges

**RANGE** Common throughout, except N Scotland and Scottish Highlands.

**FLOWERS** June–August

**SIMILAR SPECIES** Water Avens, *Geum rivale*, orange-pink to purplish nodding flowers, May–September. Scattered, especially N, rare in SE. Scattered in Ireland.

# Agrimony

*Agrimonia eupatoria*

A tall plant with large leaves, each
made up of 3–6 pairs of toothed
leaflets. The flowering heads are
long **spikes** with many yellow
flowers, each about 5–8 mm across.
Agrimony has many uses in herbal
medicine, including the treatment
of gallstones and ulcers and to stop
bleeding.

**SIZE** To 80 cm

**HABITAT** Hedgebanks, roadsides

**RANGE** Throughout, but only
scattered in Scotland

**FLOWERS** June–August

**SIMILAR SPECIES** Fragrant
Agrimony, *Agrimonia procera*;
leaves sweetly aromatic when
crushed.

A plant with pretty, soft green leaves with rounded lobes, and heads of tiny yellow-green flowers, each only 3–4 mm across. The flowers have no petals, but the yellowish **sepals** are petal-like. The name *Alchemilla* comes from the word 'alchemy'; the water drops found on the leaves after rain were gathered by alchemists and used in magic potions. Lady's Mantle has a long history of medicinal use; it was used to treat cuts.

**SIZE** To 50 cm

**HABITAT** Meadows, pastures, roadsides, up to 1200 m in hilly areas.

**RANGE** Throughout, but rare in SE England and SE Ireland

**FLOWERS** June–September

# Salad Burnet

*Sanguisorba minor*

Best identified by the **pinnate** leaves at the base of the plant. The reddish flowering stems are thin and stiff and the flowers develop in tight, rounded heads, 7–12 mm across. The female flowers are at the top, the male flowers towards the bottom. The leaves are good to eat, tasting of cucumber.

**SIZE** To 30 cm

**HABITAT** Chalk and limestone grassland

**RANGE** Common in England, rare in Scotland, rare in Wales (except N and S coasts) and local in Ireland.

**FLOWERS** April–August

**SIMILAR SPECIES** Great Burnet, *Sanguisorba officinalis*, larger with oblong, red **flowerheads**. Mainly central and N England. Mostly absent from Scotland and rare in Ireland.

Also called Wall-pepper, from the strong peppery taste of its leaves and its habit of growing on dry walls. The leaves are small, fleshy and hairless. The flowers are bright yellow and star-shaped, about 12 mm across, with 5 petals.

**SIZE** To 10 cm

**HABITAT** Dunes, dry grassland, dry rocks, walls, roofs

**RANGE** Throughout, but more scattered in Scotland

**FLOWERS** June–July

*Umbilicus rupestris*

Also called Navelwort from
the shape of the shiny, circular
leaves which have a navel-like
centre. The tubular flowers
are whitish-green, 8–10 mm
long and clustered in a long
spike.

**SIZE** To 40 cm

**HABITAT** Rocks and walls

**RANGE** W and SW England,
Wales, SW Scotland, Ireland
(especially S and W).

**FLOWERS** June–August

This plant has a **rosette** of toothed leaves at its base, and small **bulbils** (tiny bulbs). In late spring the hairy flowering stalks grow up amongst grass and reveal pretty white flowers, each about 2 cm across. After flowering and producing seed the main plant dies, leaving the bulbils near the surface of the soil. These grow into new plants the following spring.

**SIZE** To 50 cm

**HABITAT** Old grassland, especially on chalk or limestone

**RANGE** Mainly in E Britain. Rare in Ireland, where probably introduced.

**FLOWERS** April–June

# Rue-leaved Saxifrage

**SAXIFRAGE FAMILY**

100 *Saxifraga tridactylites*

A small, hairy plant with red stems. The leaves each
have 3–5 leaflets and the tiny flowers (only 4–6 mm
across) are white, with 5 petals. In dry places the
leaves may be reddish.

**SIZE** To 10 cm

**HABITAT** Dunes, dry grassland, old walls, rocks

**RANGE** Throughout England and Wales, but
rather rare and local in Scotland. In Ireland
most common in central areas and mid-west.

**FLOWERS** April–June

A strikingly handsome flower of wet places. The leaves are narrow and hairy, and the red-purple flowers are grouped in showy spikes up to about 30 cm long. A patch of Purple Loosestrife in full flower adds a splash of colour to many swampy habitats in midsummer.

**SIZE** To 1.2 m

**HABITAT** River banks, lake margins, reedswamps and marshes

**RANGE** Throughout England, Wales and Ireland. In Scotland, only common in the S and W, and absent from most of central and N Scotland.

**FLOWERS** June–August

*Epilobium hirsutum*

Our largest willowherb, with pale green, hairy stems and large pinkish-purple flowers, to over 2 cm across, each with a whitish eye. The leaves are **lanceolate**, and toothed. Its fruit **pods** are 5–8 cm long, and covered with downy hairs, releasing fluffy white seeds when ripe.

**SIZE** To 1.5 m

**HABITAT** River banks, marshes, fens

**RANGE** Throughout, except for much of central, N and W Scotland

**FLOWERS** July–August

One of the most common willowherbs, it has broad, hairless, stalked leaves. The pale pink flowers are up to 10 mm across. The fruit **pods** are 4–8 cm long, and covered with downy hairs, releasing fluffy white seeds when ripe.

**SIZE** To 60 cm

**HABITAT** Woods, hedges, roadsides, rocks, walls and as a garden weed

**RANGE** Throughout

**FLOWERS** June–August

**SIMILAR SPECIES** American Willowherb, *Epilobium ciliatum*, small pink flowers and hairy, often reddish stems.

*Chamaenerion angustifolium*

A tall plant with narrow leaves, growing spirally from tall stems. When flowering it is unmistakable, with its handsome **spikes** of large pinkish-purple flowers, each flower 2–3 cm across. As in all willowherbs, the fruit is a long pod which opens to release fluffy white seeds.

**SIZE** To 1.2 m

**HABITAT** Rocky places, scree slopes, woodland clearings, disturbed ground, industrial areas. Common coloniser of burned ground, especially in clear-felled woods.

**RANGE** Throughout, but rare in most of Ireland (except parts of NE) and in N and W Scotland.

**FLOWERS** July–September

# Enchanter's Nightshade

*Circea lutetiana*

Named after Circe, the enchantress of Greek legend who turned Odysseus' men into pigs by giving them a magic potion. A common woodland plant with rounded shiny leaves, and slender stems with small white flowers held aloft. Each flower is 4–8 mm across.

**SIZE** To 70 cm

**HABITAT** Woods, hedges and banks; shady corners of gardens

**RANGE** Throughout England, Wales, Ireland and SW Scotland. Rare in central and N Scotland

**FLOWERS** June–August

# Sanicle

*Sanicula europaea*

Sanicle has glossy, dark green toothed leaves with 3–5 lobes. The flowers are **umbels** of small pinkish flowers, each flower about 3 mm across. Later these develop into hooked fruits which cling to animal fur or clothing.

**SIZE** To 60 cm

**HABITAT** Woodland, especially beech and oak, on rich soils

**RANGE** Common, but local, throughout

**FLOWERS** May–September

Also known as Queen Anne's Lace, this is the commonest roadside member of the carrot family in southern England. The stems are hollow and the leaves rather feathery, hence the name 'Parsley'. Has abundant white, lace-like flowers in spring, each 3.5–4 mm across, in **umbels** to about 6 cm across.

**SIZE** To 1 m

**HABITAT** Roadsides, wood margins, banks

**RANGE** Throughout, but commonest in the S, and more local in SW Ireland and N and W Scotland.

**FLOWERS** April–June

Rather similar to Cow Parsley (p.107), but distinguished by its purple-spotted, hairy stems, with swollen **nodes**. Also by its solid, rather than hollow stems. Comes into flower later than Cow Parsley and Hogweed (p.111). Flowers are white, each about 2 mm across, in **umbels** to about 6 cm across. The hairy, feathery leaves have rounded segments.

**SIZE** To 1 m

**HABITAT** Hedges, banks, roadsides, woodland edges

**RANGE** Common in England and Wales. Absent from much of Scotland and Ireland, especially the N and W.

**FLOWERS** June–July

Small rather purplish **umbels**, to about 4 cm across. The leaves are feathery, dark green and hairy. The stems are rough and bristly. The latest of the common roadside members of the carrot family to come into flower, even later than Rough Chervil (p.108).

**SIZE** To 1.25 m

**HABITAT** Hedges, banks, roadsides and rough grassland

**RANGE** Throughout, but rarer in N and W Scotland

**FLOWERS** July–August

# Sweet Cicely

**CARROT FAMILY**

110 *Myrrhis odorata*

Similar to Cow Parsley (p.107), but has more
solid stems. Its leaves are even more feathery,
and fern-like with white blotches. The white
flowers grow in heads of about 5 cm across.
Smells like aniseed.

**SIZE** To 1 m

**HABITAT** Roadsides

**RANGE** Mainly in N England, N Wales
and Scotland

**FLOWERS** May–June

Tall, rather tough, bristly plant with large, lobed leaves. The **umbels** are large (to about 20 cm) and flat, with white flowers up to 10 mm across. The outer flowers have two or three larger petals.

**SIZE** To 2 m

**HABITAT** Open woods, roadside verges, grassy banks

**RANGE** Throughout

**FLOWERS** June–September

**SIMILAR SPECIES** Giant Hogweed, *Heracleum mantegazzianum*, huge, to over 5 m, with umbels to 50 cm across. Introduced, now widespread.

This speciality of the coasts has deep green, glossy leaves and yellow-green flowers (3 mm across) in spring. It tends to take the place of Cow Parsley (p.107) in the hedgerows near the sea (it is probably more sensitive to frosts, which are less frequent in coastal areas). Formerly grown as a herb, and used in cooking like Celery.

**SIZE** To 1.5 m

**HABITAT** Hedges, banks, roadsides and waste ground near the sea.

**RANGE** Scattered around coasts, especially Wales, S England and E coast of Ireland. Rare in most of Scotland.

**FLOWERS** April–June

The **pinnate** lower leaves resemble those of Salad Burnet, (p.96), hence the 'burnet' part of the name. The 'saxifrage' (p.99) part comes from its habit of growing amongst stones (sax – stone). It is in fact related to neither. The leaves are of two distinct kinds; the lower ones have 4–6 pairs of oval, toothed leaflets, the stem leaves are divided into long, narrow segments. The small **umbels** of white flowers droop when young, and are 2–5 cm across.

**SIZE** To 60 cm

**HABITAT** Dry grassland, mostly on chalk or limestone

**RANGE** Throughout, but rarer in N and W Scotland and N and W Ireland.

**FLOWERS** July–August

# Ground Elder

*Aegopodium podagraria*

Also called Bishop's Weed. This is one of the major garden weeds, and is very difficult to eradicate because of its **rhizomes** which spread quickly under the soil. The leaves are divided into three toothed leaflets and the stems are hollow. The white flowers grow in **umbels** 2–6 cm across.

**SIZE** To 1 m

**HABITAT** Waste places, gardens

**RANGE** Throughout

**FLOWERS** May–July

The leaves look a bit like Parsley, but the plant is poisonous – hence the name. The long thin, pointed green **bracts** (specialized leaves) hanging down beneath the **umbels** of small white flowers help to distinguish this species. The **umbels** are 2–6 cm across.

**SIZE** To 1.2 m

**HABITAT** A weed of waste and cultivated ground, river banks

**RANGE** Throughout lowland Britain, but only scattered and mainly coastal in Scotland. Scattered in Ireland.

**FLOWERS** July–August

# Hemlock

*Conium maculatum*

This plant's main claim to fame is that it was used by Socrates, the Greek philosopher, to poison himself. It is one of our most deadly plants, but fortunately has no attractive berries, and smells unpleasant. It is a fine-looking, tall plant with feathery leaves and a purple-blotched stem. The small white flowers are clustered in umbels 2–5 cm across.

**SIZE** To 2 m

**HABITAT** River banks, damp places and waste ground

**RANGE** Throughout the lowlands, but mainly coastal in Scotland

**FLOWERS** June–July

A tall plant, with a purplish colour and inflated leaf stalks. The divided leaves are large, to 60 cm, and have a triangular outline. The **flowerheads** are also large, up to 15 cm across, with white or pinkish flowers.

**SIZE** To 2 m

**HABITAT** Wet woodland, damp meadows, fens, marshes

**RANGE** Throughout

**FLOWERS** July–September

**SIMILAR SPECIES** Garden Angelica, *Angelica archangelica*, similar, but flowers greenish, and stems greener (and used to make confectionery).

Distinctive, with its yellow flowers, yellow-green leaves and hollow stems. The flowers grow in **umbels** which are 3–10 cm across. The leaves give off a strong smell of parsnip when crushed. Closely related to the cultivated parsnip.

**SIZE** To 1.5 m

**HABITAT** Roadside verges, dry grassland and disturbed soils, especially on chalk

**RANGE** Mainly S, central and E England

**FLOWERS** July–August

Closely related to the common vegetable, the cultivated carrot. The leaves are feathery with narrow segments, and they smell of carrot. The flowers are mostly white, but at the centre of each **umbel** (to 7 cm across) is a single red or purple flower. The fruiting heads close over into a nest-like shape after flowering. Used as a herbal medicine to treat cystitis and gout.

**SIZE** To 1 m

**HABITAT** Grassland and grassy banks, especially on chalky soils; often near the sea.

**RANGE** Throughout, but mainly coastal in Scotland

**FLOWERS** July–August

# Rock Samphire

**CARROT FAMILY**

*Crithmum maritimum*

Rock Samphire grows in tight clumps. Its **flowerheads** are greenish-yellow and grow in **umbels** measuring 3–6 cm across. The leaves are thick and succulent and can be eaten, usually when made into a pickle.

**SIZE** To 45 cm

**HABITAT** Cliffs and rocks at the coast

**RANGE** Coasts around Britain and Ireland, but absent from E coast north of Suffolk, and from NW Scotland.

**FLOWERS** July–October

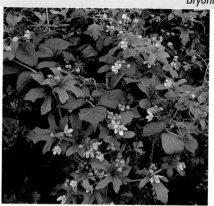

A long, climbing plant, which clings to the branches and foliage of trees and other plants using its winding **tendrils**. The leaves are lobed, and the flowers greenish-white and 10–18 mm across. Male and female flowers grow on separate plants. The female plants produce bright red, poisonous berries in the autumn.

**SIZE** To 6 m long

**HABITAT** Hedges, scrub, woodland edges

**RANGE** Central, S and E England, E Wales. Not found further N than Northumberland.

**FLOWERS** May–September

# Petty Spurge

*Euphorbia peplus*

One of the most common spurges, with green **flowerheads** (in threes) and rather blunt, oval leaves. The individual flowers are very small (a few mm across) and arranged in umbel-like groups. The stem is usually branched. Like all spurges, it has a milky, poisonous juice.

**SIZE** To 30 cm

**HABITAT** Fields, waste land and a weed in gardens

**RANGE** Throughout, but not common in much of Ireland and Scotland

**FLOWERS** May–November

**SIMILAR SPECIES** Sun Spurge, *Euphorbia helioscopia*, usually unbranched, with yellow-green flowerheads in 5s, May–October. Throughout.

The only spurge commonly found in woods. A big, handsome plant, with a tall, hairy stem. The large, yellow **flowerheads** are arranged in groups of 5–10. As with all spurges, the individual flowers are tiny (just a few mm). The leaves are long and narrow, and measure up to about 8 cm long. The stems and leaves contain a milky, poisonous juice.

**SIZE** To 80 cm

**HABITAT** Damp woodland, on rich but light soil

**RANGE** South of a line from N Wales to N Norfolk, commonest in the S. Very rare in Ireland (only on S coast).

**FLOWERS** March–May

# Dog's Mercury

**SPURGE FAMILY**

*Mercurialis perennis*

A common woodland plant with flat, oval leaves. Unlike the spurges (p.122, 123), Dog's Mercury does not have milky juice, but like those species, it is poisonous. Its flowers are 3–5 mm long, and grow in **spikes** on male plants and partly hidden by leaves on female plants. Often covers large areas of the woodland floor, and, as male and female plants are separate, big patches can be made up of one sex.

**SIZE** To 40 cm

**HABITAT** Woodland, shady rocks on mountains

**RANGE** Throughout, but rare in N and W Scotland, and in Ireland

**FLOWERS** February–April

# Heather

*Calluna vulgaris*

The dominant plant on much upland moor and heath, Heather turns whole hillsides purple when in flower. It has tough, woody stems with small opposite leaves. The flowers are small (about 4 mm long) and numerous, and both petals and sepals are pinkish-purple. Also known as Ling.

**SIZE** To 1 m

**HABITAT** Heath, moorland, bogs

**RANGE** Throughout, wherever the soils are acid

**FLOWERS** July–September

# Cross-leaved Heath

**HEATH FAMILY**

126 *Erica tetralix*

Large (to about 7 mm long), pink tubular flowers grow at the tips of the stems. The leaves are small and narrow and arranged in **whorls** of four. The whole plant is covered in soft hairs. Often grows in large patches like Heather.

**SIZE** To 60 cm

**HABITAT** Bogs, wet heaths, moorland

**RANGE** Throughout, on wet acid soils

**FLOWERS** July–September

**SIMILAR SPECIES** Bell Heather, *Erica cinerea*, is similar, but hairless and flowers purplish, 5–6 mm long. Throughout, but local in central England and central Ireland, and only on drier acid soils.

Also known as Whortleberry, Huckleberry and Blaeberry. A hairless plant with stiff shoots and finely-toothed leaves. The flowers are green and pinkish, and about 6 mm long. It has edible black berries with a grape-like waxy bloom. They are used to make jam, and yield blue and purple dye.

**SIZE** To 60 cm

**HABITAT** Heaths, moorland and woodland, on acid soils. From lowland to the tops of the mountains.

**RANGE** Found throughout, except most of the English Midlands and East Anglia.

**FLOWERS** April–June

**SIMILAR SPECIES** Cowberry, *Vaccinium vitis-idaea*, closely related. Evergreen glossy leaves, bigger pink flowers and red, edible fruits. Mainly in Scotland and mountainous N.

# Common Sea-lavender

*Limonium vulgare*

Has large, fleshy leaves and branched flowering stems. The flattish **flowerheads** are made up of many small flowers (each 6–8 mm long) and are a beautiful shade of pale purple. When dried the flowers keep their colour well, and are often used in dried flower arrangements.

**SIZE** To 35 cm

**HABITAT** Saltmarshes and coastal mud

**RANGE** Coasts of Britain, but absent from most of Scotland, and absent from Ireland.

**FLOWERS** July–October

Also called Sea Pink. A favourite seaside plant with heads of pretty pink flowers, 8–9 mm across, growing up on tall, leafless stalks out of a cushion of narrow leaves.

**SIZE** To 30 cm

**HABITAT** Saltmarshes, seaside pastures, cliffs and rocks. Also on mountains, particularly in Scotland.

**RANGE** Throughout

**FLOWERS** April–October

One of the best-known spring flowers, with pretty, pale yellow flowers, with darker orange centres, each about 3 cm across. Several flowers emerge singly from the centre of a **rosette** of leaves. Leaves are oval with rather wrinkled edges. Sometimes crosses with Cowslip (p.131) to produce spectacular hybrids with clusters of large flowers at the top of the flower-stalk.

**SIZE** To 10 cm

**HABITAT** Woodland, under hedges, on railway banks and sometimes in grassland.

**RANGE** Common throughout, but local in S and central Ireland (sometimes common where it does occur).

**FLOWERS** December–May

**SIMILAR SPECIES** Oxlip, *Primula elatior*

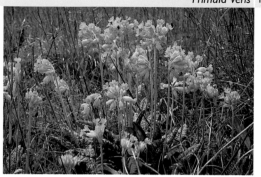

A well-known spring-flowering species. The deep yellow flowers are 10–15 mm across and grow in nodding clusters on tall stalks. The leaves are oval with rather wrinkled edges, like those of the Primrose (p.130), but narrow more abruptly into stalk. Tea made from the flowers is said to be good for insomnia, nervous tension and headaches.

**SIZE** To 20 cm

**HABITAT** Meadows, pastures, grassy banks and roadsides.

**RANGE** Locally common throughout, but has disappeared from some areas with the removal of grassland. Rarer in W and N Scotland, N Ireland, and coasts of S Ireland.

**FLOWERS** April–May

A low-growing, hairless plant with oval, pointed leaves. The yellow flowers with five **corolla lobes** are star-shaped and measure up to 12 mm across. There is a darker yellow spot at the centre of each flower.

**SIZE** To 40 cm long

**HABITAT** Woods, shady hedges

**RANGE** Throughout, although rare in parts of East Anglia

**FLOWERS** May–September

A low-growing plant which creeps along the ground. Resembles Yellow Pimpernel (p.132), but its yellow flowers are more cup-shaped and bigger (15–25 mm across), and its leaves rounded, rather than pointed.

**SIZE** Only a few cm high, but creeps for 60 cm.

**HABITAT** Hedges, grassy banks; often planted as a garden flower and escapes.

**RANGE** Commonest in England and Wales, N to S Scotland. Absent from central and N Scotland. Scattered in Ireland, mainly in N.

**FLOWERS** June–August

# Yellow Loosestrife

134 *Lysimachia vulgaris*

A much taller plant than
Yellow Pimpernel (p.132)
and Creeping Jenny (p.133),
with upright growth. The
flowers are bright yellow,
about 15 mm across, and
are clustered together on
flowering **spikes**. The
narrow leaves are arranged
in opposite pairs or in
**whorls** around the stem.

**SIZE** To 1.5 m

**HABITAT** River banks, fens,
marshes, lake sides

**RANGE** Scattered throughout, but
not in N and NW Scotland

**FLOWERS** July–August

# Chickweed Wintergreen

*Trientalis europaea* 135

A slender plant with a **whorl** of oval leaves and a single star-shaped white flower, usually with seven petals. The flower is 15–18 mm across and grows at the end of a thin stalk about 5 cm tall.

**SIZE** To 25 cm

**HABITAT** Pine woods, mossy grassland and bogs

**RANGE** Mainly Scotland, but also S to Derbyshire and Suffolk (rare)

**FLOWERS** June–July

Also called Shepherd's Weatherglass because the flowers close up in bad weather. A widespread plant with pretty red flowers. It is hairless and has square stems and oval leaves. The five-petalled, red or pink (rarely blue) flowers are up to 14 mm across.

**SIZE** To 30 cm

**HABITAT** An arable weed, usually near cultivated land; also on dunes.

**RANGE** Throughout, but only scattered and mainly coastal in Scotland.

**FLOWERS** June–August

**SIMILAR SPECIES** Bog Pimpernel, *Anagallis tenella*, is related; delicate and creeping; flowers pale pink (June–August) and leaves round. Boggy places, commonest in W.

A creeping, hairless plant with fleshy, mostly opposite, leaves. There are no petals, but the **calyx** is coloured and forms the flower. The flowers are pink or pinkish-white, and about 5 mm across.

**SIZE** To 30 cm

**HABITAT** Saltmarsh, coastal grassland, coastal rocks; some inland sites on salty soils.

**RANGE** Around all coasts

**FLOWERS** June–August

The pink flowers (each 10–15 mm across) grow together in rather flat-topped clusters. The oval leaves at the base of the plant form a **rosette**. Used in herbal medicine to treat anaemia, rheumatism and gout.

**SIZE** To 50 cm

**HABITAT** Dunes, dry grassland

**RANGE** Throughout, but mainly coastal in Scotland and absent from N Scotland.

**FLOWERS** June–October

**SIMILAR SPECIES** Lesser Centaury, *Centaurium pulchellum*

A hairless plant with pairs of opposite leaves joined around the stem. The flowers are clustered, rather like those of Common Centaury (p.138), but in this case they are bright yellow. Each flower has 8 petals and is about 8–15 mm long.

**SIZE** To 45 cm

**HABITAT** Dunes and chalk and limestone grassland

**RANGE** Mainly S and central England, N and S coasts of Wales, central Ireland.

**FLOWERS** June–October

Also known as Felwort, this is our most common gentian. The flowers are long (12–18 mm) and tube-like, opening out at the top into five lobes. They do not appear until late summer or autumn, and are usually dull purple (sometimes white). The leaves are **lanceolate** and pointed.

**SIZE** To 25 cm

**HABITAT** Chalk and limestone grassland, dunes

**RANGE** Throughout, but rare in most of W Scotland and N Ireland

**FLOWERS** August–October

**SIMILAR SPECIES** Field Gentian, *Gentianella campestris*, similar but 4-lobed flowers bluish-lilac (white), July–October. Dunes and grassland, mainly Scotland and Lake District. N and W Ireland

Unmistakable, with its large, rather shiny leaves each with three leaflets, rather like those of beans (hence the name). The flowers grow together on a single stalk and are pink on the outside and white inside. Each flower is about 15 mm across and has five lobes with fringed edges. Extracts of bogbean are used to treat indigestion.

**SIZE** To 40 cm

**HABITAT** Bogs, fens, pond and lake edges; usually in acid water.

**RANGE** Throughout, but commonest in N and W

**FLOWERS** May–June

An upright plant with rather tough stems. Its long, hairy leaves resemble dogs' tongues – hence its name. The flowers are small (5–6 mm across) and maroon, growing clustered together. The leaves are **lanceolate** and when crushed have a sharp, unpleasant smell. Later in the season these are replaced by hooked fruits which cling to animal fur or clothing.

**SIZE** To 1 m

**HABITAT** Grassy areas on dry soils, dunes

**RANGE** Mainly lowland England and Wales. Absent from most of Ireland and Scotland, except parts of S and E coasts.

**FLOWERS** June–August

This tall, hairy plant is characteristic of river banks. It has drooping clusters of pale yellow (sometimes purplish or pink) flowers, each about 12–18 mm long. Folknames such as Boneset, Knitbone and Bruisewort tell of long medicinal use for this herb – its juice promotes the growth of connective tissue and bone. The photograph above shows the similar Russian Comfrey, *Symphytum* x *uplandicum*, the most common roadside comfrey, with purple-violet or red-pink flowers and rough hairs.

**SIZE** To 1.2 m

**HABITAT** River and stream banks, wet ditches, fens and marshes

**RANGE** Throughout

**FLOWERS** May–September

# Common Forget-me-not

*Myosotis arvensis*

Also known as Field Forget-me-not. Our most common forget-me-not, it has very small, bright blue flowers (to about 5 mm across). The leaves are **lanceolate** and both stem and leaves have spreading hairs.

**SIZE** To 30 cm

**HABITAT**
Fields, woodland edge, roadsides, waste ground, dunes

**RANGE** Throughout

**FLOWERS** April–September

**SIMILAR SPECIES** Wood Forget-me-not, *Myosotis sylvatica*, similar but larger flowers (about 8mm). Damp woods, also common garden-escape. Mainly central and E England and S Scotland. May–September.

# Water Forget-me-not

*Myosotis scorpioides*

A large-flowered species (compared to the Common Forget-me-not p.144) of wet places. The flowers are about 8 mm across. The lower leaves are up to 7 cm long and oblong or **lanceolate**. The upper leaves are narrower.

**SIZE** To 45 cm

**HABITAT** Banks of rivers, streams and ponds

**RANGE** Throughout

**FLOWERS** May–September

**SIMILAR SPECIES** Tufted Forget-me-not, *Myosotis laxa*

# Viper's Bugloss

*Echium vulgare*

A very handsome plant when in full flower, with its tall **spikes** of vivid blue flowers (pink in bud). Each flower is 10–20 mm long. The deep flowers are particularly attractive to bees, butterflies and moths. The fruits are said to look like a viper's head, hence the name.

**SIZE** To 1 m

**HABITAT** Light, mostly sandy soils, dunes or coastal cliffs

**RANGE** Scattered throughout, but absent from most of N and NW Scotland, and only along the E coast of Ireland.

**FLOWERS** June–September

# Hedge Bindweed

*Calystegia sepium* 147

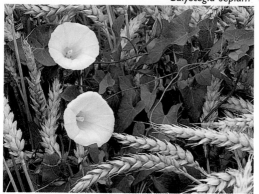

The smaller flowered of the two large bindweeds
(see also Large Bindweed, p.148). Like the
other bindweeds, the flowers are large and
funnel-shaped, in this case pure white
(occasionally pink), and up to 7 cm long.
Climbs by twining around other plants or
fences. The leaves are up to 15 cm long and
heart-shaped.

**SIZE** To 3 m

**HABITAT** Fens, wet woodland, hedges; also a
garden weed.

**RANGE** Throughout, mainly in lowlands

**FLOWERS** July–September

# Large Bindweed

148 *Calystegia silvatica*

An introduction from SE Europe, via gardens. Like Hedge Bindweed (p.147), but has even bigger white (occasionally pink), funnel-shaped flowers up to 9 cm long. The 2 **bracts** (special leaves) at the flower-base are swollen, and hide the **calyx**. Climbs up stems and twigs of other plants by twining. The leaves are large and heart-shaped.

**SIZE** To 3 m

**HABITAT** Waste ground, hedges and fences, gardens

**RANGE** Throughout, especially in England and Wales

**FLOWERS** July–September

**BINDWEED FAMILY**

# Sea Bindweed

*Calystegia soldanella* 149

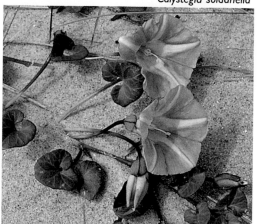

Spreads by means of **runners** through the sand. The leaves are rounded and rather heart-shaped. The flowers are pink with five pale stripes, and about 5 cm long.

**SIZE** To 60 cm long (low-growing)

**HABITAT** Sandy or shingly coasts, dunes

**RANGE** All around coasts, but rarer in NE, and absent from N and E Scotland

**FLOWERS** June–August

# Field Bindweed

*Convolvulus arvensis*

**BINDWEED FAMILY**

The leaves of this bindweed are shaped like a spear-head. The flowers are small (to about 2 cm long) and white, or pink with pale stripes. They are strongly scented and attract many insects as a result. Spreads quickly by underground stems.

**SIZE** To 75 cm, but often low-growing (creeps over the ground rather than growing upwards).

**HABITAT** Hedges, farmland, roadsides; also a persistent garden weed with deep, underground stems.

**RANGE** Throughout England and Wales, but rarer in Scotland; widespread in Ireland.

**FLOWERS** June–September

# Woody Nightshade ✿

Also known as Bittersweet as the dried stems, used in medicine, taste bitter but sweeten with age. The most common wild nightshade, with distinctive flowers (15 mm), the purple petals surrounding yellow **anthers**. The fruits are poisonous, oval berries, turning from green, to yellow, to red when ripe. The leaves are either oval and pointed, or have a large lobe at the end and two smaller side lobes.

**SIZE** To 2 m (scrambles rather than climbs)

**HABITAT** Hedges, woods, waste ground, shingle beaches.

**RANGE** Throughout, mainly lowlands; rather rare in N and W Scotland.

**FLOWERS** June–September

# Black Nightshade

152 *Solanum nigrum*

In general shape and size, Black Nightshade resembles the Potato, which belongs to the same family. The flowers are white with yellow anthers, and about 5 mm across. The fruits turn from green to black when ripe, and are poisonous. The leaves are oval and pointed, to about 6 cm long.

**SIZE** To 60 cm

**HABITAT** A weed of gardens and waste ground

**RANGE** Lowland England and Wales, most common in the S and E.

**FLOWERS** July–September

# Deadly Nightshade

*Atropa belladonna* 153

**SIZE** To 1.3 m

**HABITAT** Light woods, scrub, hedges on chalky soils; also sometimes around old buildings.

**RANGE** Scattered, mainly central and E England

**FLOWERS** June–September

This deadly, bushy plant is particularly dangerous because its ripe berries, shiny, black and cherry-sized, look so attractive, but are in fact very poisonous. The purple flowers droop and are 2.5–3 cm long, the leaves oval, pointed and up to 20 cm. The name *belladonna* comes from the practice, once common in Italy, of using an extract of the berry to enlarge the pupil of the eye, thus enhancing beauty (*bella* = 'beautiful', *donna* = 'woman'). An extract, atropine, is still used today to enlarge the pupil in eye examinations.

# Henbane

Henbane

NIGHTSHADE FAMILY

154 *Hyoscyamus niger*

A tall plant with large, felty, oval leaves. The flowers, which develop in a cluster at the top of the plant, are yellow, with purple veins. Each is 2–3 cm across. Like Deadly Nightshade (p.153), Henbane is a very poisonous plant, but does not have attractive berries.

SIZE To 80 cm

HABITAT Waste ground, farmyards, old habitations, sandy soils near the coast. The seeds live for a long time in the ground, and germinate if the soil is disturbed.

RANGE Scattered, mainly in S and E Britain

FLOWERS June–August

# Great Mullein

*Verbascum thapsus* 155

Also called Aaron's Rod, because of its straight, staff-like growth. It is a tall plant, covered in soft woolly hairs, with large, oval leaves forming a **rosette** at its base. A single, leafy flowering stem rises up from the centre, bearing a **spike** of yellow flowers, each flower 15–35 mm across. Used as a herbal remedy for coughs and asthma.

**SIZE** To 2 m

**HABITAT** Banks, roadsides and waste ground on light soils. Likes warm, sunny spots.

**RANGE** Throughout, but rarer in N and W Scotland

**FLOWERS** June–August

**SIMILAR SPECIES** Dark Mullein, *Verbascum nigrum*, smaller, less hairy, leaves heart-shaped. S and E England.

# Common Toadflax

156  *Linaria vulgaris*

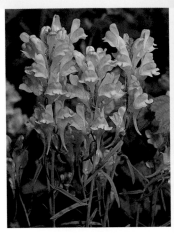

The toadflaxes have unusual flowers which look rather like Snapdragons. Each flower has an upper and a lower lip. The lower lip is divided into three lobes and closes over the mouth of the flower. This species has narrow leaves, up to 8 cm long, which grow in **whorls** around the stem. The flowers are bright yellow and orange, each 2–3 cm long, with a straight **spur**.

**SIZE** To 80 cm

**HABITAT** Roadsides, grassy banks, hedges and waste land

**RANGE** Throughout, but rare in N and W Scotland, and only scattered in Ireland

**FLOWERS** July–October

# Ivy-leaved Toadflax

*Cymbalaria muralis* 157

Originally a garden plant, but now well established in wild habitats as well, particularly in the cracks of walls in towns and houses. Also found rooted in crevices and trailing over rocks. The flowers are lilac coloured, 10–15 mm across, and the leaves are shaped like Ivy leaves.

**SIZE** To 80 cm (trailing)

**HABITAT** Walls, rocks

**RANGE** Throughout, but rare in N and NW Scotland

**FLOWERS** May–September

A well-known and easily recognized wild flower. The tall flower **spike** has up to 80 tube-shaped individual flowers, each up to 5 cm long. The flowers are usually pink, more rarely white. The leaves are oval and pointed, measuring up to 30 cm long. Foxgloves are a source of drugs for the treatment of heart disorders.

**SIZE** To 1.5 m

**HABITAT** Woodland clearings, heaths, rocky outcrops, on acid soils

**RANGE** Throughout, but rather rare in the East Anglian fenland and chalky areas of SE England.

**FLOWERS** June–September

One of the largest of the common speedwells. The flowers are bright blue with a white centre, and about 10 mm across. The leaves are hairy and heart-shaped, with serrated edges.

**SIZE** To 25 cm

**HABITAT** Woodland, hedges, banks and grassland

**RANGE** Throughout

**FLOWERS** March–July

A creeping plant with hairy stems which root at intervals as they spread out along the ground. The long-stalked flowering heads grow upright from the low-growing stems. The heads are made up of between 15 and 25 lilac flowers, each about 8 mm across. Its leaves are oval and hairy, with shallow teeth.

**SIZE** To 15 cm

**HABITAT** Heaths, dry grassland and open woods

**RANGE** Throughout

**FLOWERS** May–August

**SIMILAR SPECIES** Wood Speedwell, *Veronica montana*

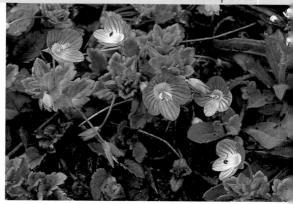

A common weed of cultivated fields, introduced in the 1820s from Asia. It has straggly growth and rather triangular leaves. The flowers are bright blue and 8–12 mm across, with a pale lower lip formed by the lower lobe of the corolla.

**SIZE** To 10 cm

**HABITAT** Cultivated areas

**RANGE** Throughout, but rarer in N and W Scotland

**FLOWERS** January–December

**SIMILAR SPECIES** Grey Field Speedwell, *Veronica polita*

This slender, creeping species was introduced and is now
common, especially in lawns where its abundant flowers
can form pale blue patches in spring. The lilac-blue
flowers, 8–10 mm across, grow on very thin stems.
The leaves are small, to 10 mm, and rounded. Any
broken piece of this plant can root, so it
continues to grow well in lawns even when
mown regularly.

**SIZE** To 5 cm

**HABITAT** Lawns, gardens, grass verges and
grazed meadows

**RANGE** Scattered throughout

**FLOWERS** March–July

A common plant with a weak, straggly, trailing growth. The leaves are ivy-shaped and hairy. The flowers are small, 4–5 mm across, and pale blue or white.

**SIZE** To 10 cm

**HABITAT** A weed of cultivated and waste ground

**RANGE** Throughout England, Wales and S and E Scotland. Rare in N and W Scotland, scattered and local in Ireland.

**FLOWERS** March–August

# Thyme-leaved Speedwell

FIGWORT FAMILY

*Veronica serpyllifolia*

A common speedwell with oblong, shiny leaves. The flowering stems end in a cluster of small pale blue or white flowers with darker veins. Each flower is between 6–8 mm across.

**SIZE** To 10 cm

**HABITAT** Grassland, heaths, waste and cultivated land

**RANGE** Throughout

**FLOWERS** April–September

This is an upright growing, small speedwell, covered in soft hairs. The tiny blue flowers are about 3 mm across and grow in the leaf **axils**. The leaves are triangular and toothed.

**SIZE** To 20 cm (variable and often much smaller)

**HABITAT** Cultivated and waste land, heaths, rock-ledges, wall tops

**RANGE** Throughout

**FLOWERS** March–October

This speedwell grows in shallow water or in wet marshy ground. It has long, oval, rather fleshy leaves. Paired flowering stalks grow up from the leaf **axils**, and each has a cluster of flowers at the end. The flowers are blue and up to 7 mm across. The leaves can be eaten in salads as an alternative to watercress.

**SIZE** To 60 cm

**HABITAT** Wet meadows, streams, ponds

**RANGE** Throughout, but rare in NW Scotland

**FLOWERS** May–September

The pink flowers of Lousewort are up to 2.5 cm long and very striking, with their overarching hoods. They grow up from a mat of deeply divided leaves. Like several other members of this family, this plant is semi-parasitic: it lives attached to the roots of other species from which it gains part of its food.

**SIZE** To 20 cm

**HABITAT** Damp heaths, moors, bogs

**RANGE** Throughout, but commoner in the N and W

**FLOWERS** April–July

**SIMILAR SPECIES** Marsh Lousewort, *Pedicularis palustris*, more upright, flowers 2 cm and purplish-pink. Wet heaths and bogs, May–September.

# Yellow-rattle

*Rhinanthus minor*

An upright plant with tough stems and opposite, rather long, toothed leaves. The flowers are large (to 15 mm long) and yellow and have an inflated **calyx**.
When ripe, the seeds rattle inside the fruiting head – hence the name. It is a semi-parasite, attaching itself to the roots of other species from which it gains nourishment.

**SIZE** To 50 cm

**HABITAT** Damp grassland, particularly permanent pasture and hay meadows

**RANGE** Throughout

**FLOWERS** May–September

This plant has long, thin leaves, and yellow flowers which grow in pairs up the stems. The flowers, each about 10–18 mm long, all face the same way. It is semi-parasitic, living attached to the roots of other plants from which it gains food.

**SIZE** To 60 cm

**HABITAT** Dry woodland, heaths

**RANGE** Scattered throughout, but rarer in E England and in much of Ireland.

**FLOWERS** May–October

There are many species of eyebright, all difficult to distinguish. But as a group they are quite easy to recognize. They are small plants, usually growing amongst grasses, with bright flowers clustered together on leafy stems. Each flower is about 5–10 mm long, lilac or white, often with a yellow centre.

The leaves are oval and toothed; opposite towards the base of the plant, but alternate towards the top. Eyebrights are used to treat sore eyes, nasal congestion and catarrh. They are semi-parasites, living attached to the roots of other plants in order to gain nourishment.

**SIZE** To 40 cm

**HABITAT** Grassland, heaths, woodland edges

**RANGE** Scattered throughout

**FLOWERS** June–September

A rather scruffy-looking, hairy plant with a purplish tinge to its stems and leaves. The purple-pink flowers (each 8–10 mm long) grow bent over to one side. A semi-parasite living attached to the roots of other plants for food.

**SIZE** To 50 cm

**HABITAT** Cultivated fields, waste places, open grassland

**RANGE** Throughout, but mainly coastal in central and N Scotland

**FLOWERS** June–August

# Water Mint

*Mentha aquatica*

Like nearly all mints, this species smells strongly when crushed. The lilac flowers are clumped in rounded heads near the tops of the stems. The stems have a distinct red colour, and the leaves are oval, toothed and rather shiny. Mints contain aromatic oils useful for treating indigestion and colds.

**SIZE** To 1 m

**HABITAT** Marshes, wet woods, stream sides, ponds

**RANGE** Throughout

**FLOWERS** July–October

# Corn Mint

## *Mentha arvensis*

Unlike Water Mint (p.172), this
is a plant of rather drier places.
It is also unusual in not having an
obvious minty smell. The
flowers (each 3–4 mm long)
grow in clusters lower down
the stem rather than at the top.
The leaves are rather long, and
hairy on both sides.

**SIZE** To 60 cm

**HABITAT** Arable fields, woodland
clearings, waste ground

**RANGE** Throughout, but mainly in lowlands

**FLOWERS** May–October

**SIMILAR SPECIES** Spearmint, *Mentha
spicata*, commonest garden mint, also wild.
Leaves pointed and hairless. Flowers lilac,
pink or white spikes July–September. Scattered,
rare in Ireland.

*Lycopus europaeus*

Once used as a source of black dye by gypsies, hence the name.
Looks like a large mint (see Water Mint and Corn Mint p.172 and
p.173), but is almost unscented, and the leaf margins are deeply cut.
The flowers are small (about 3 mm across) and white.

**SIZE** To 1 m

**HABITAT** River banks, ditches, marshes

**RANGE** Throughout lowlands, but more scattered in N Scotland
and Ireland.

**FLOWERS** June–September

Marjoram is a well-known herb, with a strongly aromatic smell and taste, used as a flavouring for food. It has a bushy growth and a purple tinge to the stem and leaves. The leaves are rather small, to 4 cm long. The flowers are 6–8 mm long, grow in a mint-like cluster (see p.172), and are a pretty shade of pink-purple.

**SIZE** To 80 cm

**HABITAT** Dry grassland, hedges and scrub, on chalky soils

**RANGE** Scattered throughout, but absent from central, N and W Scotland. Commonest in the south.

**FLOWERS** July–September

# Wild Basil

**MINT FAMILY**

*Clinopodium vulgare*

A well-known edible herb with a distinct flavour, but much less strongly aromatic than Marjoram (p.175) (although cultivated basil has a strong flavour). Resembles Marjoram, but lacks the purple tinge to the stem and leaves. Both stem and leaves are covered in soft hairs. The leaves are long and oval. The pink-purple flowers, each 12–20 mm long, are clustered at the tip of the stem and at the leaf bases lower down.

**SIZE** To 80 cm

**HABITAT** Hedges, scrub on dry, chalky soils

**RANGE** Mainly lowland England and Wales; Scattered in S and E Scotland, and SE Ireland.

**FLOWERS** July–September

# Basil Thyme

*Acinos arvensis*

This species is rather like Wild Basil (p.176), but with
smaller leaves (to 15 mm), and larger than Wild
Thyme (p.178). Basil Thyme has violet or blue
flowers, with white markings, each to about 10 mm
long. The flowers are not as tightly clustered as those of
Wild Basil. Despite its name it is not often used as a herb.

**SIZE** To 20 cm

**HABITAT** Arable fields, dry grassland, on chalky soils

**RANGE** Mainly S and SE England; scattered in SE Ireland

**FLOWERS** May–September

Wild Thyme has a mat-like growth, with creeping, branched, rather woody stems and small oval leaves. The leaves give off the characteristic thyme smell when crushed. The small pink-purple (sometimes white) flowers are about 3–4 mm long and clustered at the tips of the flowering shoots. A well-known herb for flavouring food, although the species usually used in cooking is the stronger Garden Thyme *Thymus vulgaris*, a native of South Europe, often grown here in gardens.

**SIZE** To 7 cm

**HABITAT** Dry grassland, heaths, dunes, rocks

**RANGE** Throughout

**FLOWERS** May–August

A common, large plant of shady hedgerows, with a characteristic unpleasant smell when crushed. The leaves are large and tapering, with distinctly toothed edges. The flowers are deep reddish-pink and 12–18 mm long. Woundworts have a medicinal reputation – bruised leaves are said to stop bleeding and promote healing.

**SIZE** To 1 m

**HABITAT** Woods, shady hedges

**RANGE** Throughout

**FLOWERS** July–August

**SIMILAR SPECIES** Betony, *Stachys officinalis*, close relation with spikes of purple-red flowers and a **rosette** of heart-shaped, toothed leaves. Woods, grassland, heath, England and Wales, June–September.

# Black Horehound

*Ballota nigra*

Looks rather like a tall, straggly dead-nettle (see Red Dead-nettle p.182), but the leaves have a nasty smell. The **flowerheads** are tight clusters of purple flowers, each about 15 mm long. The leaves have coarse teeth and are oval or heart-shaped.

**SIZE** To 1 m

**HABITAT** Hedges, banks, roadsides

**RANGE** Mainly England and Wales,
in lowland sites

**FLOWERS** June–October

**SIMILAR SPECIES** White Horehound,
*Marrubium vulgare*

One of our prettiest wild flowers, with loose clusters of large white, hooded flowers, each 20–25 mm long. The lip of the flower provides a convenient landing stage for visiting bees and other insects which pollinate the flowers. The toothed leaves are heart-shaped and pointed. Dead-nettles are so called because their leaves look like nettle leaves, but they do not sting.

**SIZE** To 60 cm

**HABITAT** Hedges, waste land and arable fields, gardens

**RANGE** Throughout, but rare or local in N and W and probably only introduced in Ireland.

**FLOWERS** May–December

Like White Dead-nettle (p.181), another common dead-nettle, but a smaller plant with pink-purple flowers, each 10–15 mm long. The leaves are hairy and heart-shaped, with rounded teeth; they resemble those of Stinging Nettle, but do not sting.

**SIZE** To 45 cm

**HABITAT** Waste land and arable fields, gardens

**RANGE** Throughout

**FLOWERS** March–October

**SIMILAR SPECIES** Henbit Dead-nettle, *Lamium amplexicaule*, similar flowers, but leaves joined in pairs round stem. E Britain.

A beautiful, tall woodland plant, which spreads by long, leafy **runners**. The leaves are like those of dead-nettles (p.181) and the flowers large (17–20 mm long), hooded and bright yellow.

**SIZE** To 60 cm

**HABITAT** Damp woods on heavier soils

**RANGE** Mainly England and Wales

**FLOWERS** May–June

This fine plant has large, hooded flowers which are blue-violet in colour and up to 2 cm long. They grow in pairs, pointing in the same direction. The leaves are oval and slightly toothed.

**SIZE** To 50 cm

**HABITAT** Streamsides, fens, water meadows

**RANGE** Throughout, but rare in E Scotland, and in Ireland

**FLOWERS** June–September

**SIMILAR SPECIES** Lesser Skullcap, *Scutellaria minor*, smaller, pink-purple flowers, 6–10 mm. Mainly S and W, usually wet, acid soils. July–October.

A pale green, hairy plant with oval, rather crinkled leaves and an aromatic smell. The yellow-green flowers grow in tall **spikes**. The individual flowers are quite small, about 8 mm long, with a five-lobed lip. It is not closely related to edible sage, and not used as a herb.

**SIZE** To 30 cm

**HABITAT** Woods, heaths, grassland, dunes, rocks; on rather dry, acid soils.

**RANGE** Throughout, but rather rare in parts of central England and E Anglia and in central Ireland.

**FLOWERS** July–September

Selfheal has dense **spikes** of violet flowers on short erect stems. Each flower is 10–15 mm long, and hooded. The leaves are oval and stalked. The common name indicates traditional herbal use, and indeed this flower contains oils used for treating sore throats.

**SIZE** To 30 cm

**HABITAT** Grassland, clearings in woods, lawns

**RANGE** Throughout

**FLOWERS** June–September

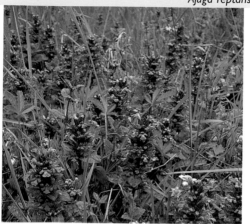

Resembles Selfheal (p.186) with its **spikes** of flowers, but the flowers are blue, about 15 mm long and not hooded. The base leaves are stalked and 50 mm long, the unstalked stem leaves grow in pairs. Spreads freely by long, leafy runners.

**SIZE** To 40 cm

**HABITAT** Wet woods, meadows

**RANGE** Throughout

**FLOWERS** May–July

*Glechoma hederacea*

A small, common plant, with long, creeping
and rooting stems and rounded, hairy leaves.
The flowers (each 15–20 mm long) are violet
and have purple spots on the lower lip.

**SIZE** To 30 cm, but often smaller

**HABITAT** Grassland, waste places, woods

**RANGE** Throughout, but rare in N Scotland

**FLOWERS** March–May

Perhaps one of the most attractive of all our wild
flowers. The delicate, pale blue (rarely white) bell-
shaped flowers, each 12–20 mm long, are held up
on thin stalks and sway in the breeze. The leaves at
the base of the plant are rounded and long-stalked,
while the stem leaves are thin and grass-like. This
species is called Bluebell in Scotland, (see also the
species more usually called Bluebell on p.242).

**SIZE** To 50 cm

**HABITAT** Dry grassland, heaths

**RANGE** Throughout; in Ireland only common in N and W

**FLOWERS** July–September

*Campanula glomerata*

This species has short, hairy stems with clusters of purple-blue (rarely white) bell-shaped flowers, held upright. Each flower is up to 2.5 cm long. The base leaves are oval and long-stalked, the stem leaves unstalked.

**SIZE** To 20 cm

**HABITAT** Chalk grassland

**RANGE** Mainly S and E England, also SE Scotland. Absent from Ireland.

**FLOWERS** May–September

# Giant Bellflower

*Campanula latifolia* 191

A tall plant, with rather bushy growth and hairy stems and leaves. The flowers, which are purplish-blue (sometimes white), are big (to about 4 cm long). The base leaves are up to 20 cm long and the stem leaves narrow to a sharp point.

**SIZE** To 1.2 m

**HABITAT** Woods, hedges, banks

**RANGE** Scattered in Britain, mainly in the N of England, rare in S England and N Scotland.

**FLOWERS** July–August

A slightly smaller version of Giant Bellflower (p.191). The flowers are smaller (to about 3.5 cm) and slightly darker blue. The base leaves are about 10 cm long; the stem leaves resemble those of the Stinging Nettle in shape.

**SIZE** To 1 m

**HABITAT** Woods and hedges

**RANGE** Mainly S and E England and E Wales. A few localities in SE Ireland. Not in N England or Scotland.

**FLOWERS** July–September

This species has small heads of tightly packed, bright blue flowers. The **flowerheads** are about 3.5 cm across, the individual flowers 5 mm long. The leaves are small and oblong, and all grow low down on the stem. It looks a bit like a scabious (see Field Scabious, p.205 and Small Scabious, p.206). Sometimes found on sheep pasture, hence the common name.

**SIZE** To 50 cm

**HABITAT** Dry, acid grassland and dunes

**RANGE** Mainly in the W of Britain and Ireland

**FLOWERS** June–August

A familiar garden weed which climbs up other plants. The flowers are greenish-white and tiny, only about 2 mm across. The leaves are long and narrow, with prickly edges. Also called Cleavers because of the clinging, hooked hairs which cover the leaves and stem, and because of the round hooked fruits which stick to clothing and animal fur. Used to make natural shampoo and deodorants. Also used in medicine to treat urinary infections and skin disease.

**SIZE** To 1.2 m

**HABITAT** Found in many habitats, from woodland and gardens, to shingle and waste ground.

**RANGE** Throughout

**FLOWERS** June–August

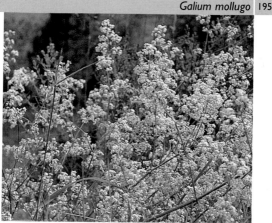

A large bedstraw common in hedgerows, it has clusters of small,
white flowers, each flower about 3 mm across. The
stems are smooth and the leaves grow in **whorls**
of 6–8. Climbs up shrubs in hedges and wood
margins. The fruits are hairless, not clinging like
those of Goosegrass (p.194).

**SIZE** To 1.2 m

**HABITAT** Hedges, scrub, woodland

**RANGE** Scattered throughout, but commonest in
lowland England. Only scattered in Scotland and Ireland.

**FLOWERS** July–August

# Lady's Bedstraw

*Galium verum*

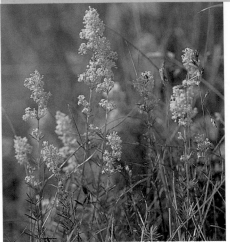

A very distinctive plant, with its soft clusters of bright yellow flowers which smell of hay. Each flower is 2–3 mm across. The leaves are narrow, dark green and in **whorls** of 8–12. Often creeps amongst grasses, sending up tall flowering stems in summer. Its fruits are smooth and about 1.5 mm across.

**SIZE** To 1 m

**HABITAT** Grassland, hedges, dunes

**RANGE** Throughout

**FLOWERS** July–August

A woodland plant with relatively large flowers for a bedstraw, each about 6 mm across. The flowers are white and grow in clusters at the top of the stems. The leaves grow in **whorls** of 6–8 and have prickly edges. The fruits are 3 mm across and have hooked bristles. The whole plant is sweet-scented, especially when dried. Sometimes called Sweet Woodruff.

**SIZE** To 45 cm

**HABITAT** Woods on damp, usually chalky, soils

**RANGE** Throughout

**FLOWERS** May–June

The entire plant of Crosswort is yellow-green and the flowers, each 2–3 mm across, are yellow. The leaves are oval and arranged in **whorls** of four like a cross, hence the name.

**SIZE** To 70 cm

**HABITAT** Meadows, open woods, scrub, usually on chalky soils

**RANGE** England and Wales, to S Scotland. Not in Ireland.

**FLOWERS** May–June

This species has a low, mat-like growth, and leaves arranged in **whorls** of 6–8. The flowering stems grow up and end in a cluster of white flowers, each about 3 mm across.

**SIZE** To 25 cm

**HABITAT** Heaths, acid grassland, moorland

**RANGE** Throughout

**FLOWERS** June–August

# Common Marsh Bedstraw

**BEDSTRAW FAMILY**

200 *Galium palustre*

The common bedstraw of wet habitats, it climbs up stems of other marsh plants such as reeds and rushes. The short, blunt leaves grow in **whorls** of 4–6. The white flowers are about 3–4 mm across.

**SIZE** To 35 cm

**HABITAT** Marshes, fens and ditches; usually in places which dry out each season.

**RANGE** Throughout

**FLOWERS** June–August

**SIMILAR SPECIES** Fen Bedstraw, *Galium uliginosum*, similar, but sharp-pointed leaves (whorls of 6–8) and smaller flowers. Not N Scotland or N Ireland. July–August.

A very well known woody climber, with large heads of yellow and
pink flowers. Each flower is shaped like a tube, with the **stamens**
sticking out, and is 3–5 cm long. The flowers are sweet-smelling and
attract moths and other insects. The fruits are
bright red berries.

**SIZE** 1 o 6 m

**HABITAT** Woods, hedges, scrub, also on
rocks in some places

**RANGE** Throughout

**FLOWERS** June–September

*Valeriana officinalis*

A tall plant with opposite, **pinnate** leaves and heads of small, pale pink flowers, each 2.5–5 mm long. One of its alternative names is All-heal, and it is indeed used medicinally, to treat nervous tension, insomnia and headaches.

**SIZE** To 1.5 m

**HABITAT** Rough grassland, scrub, wood margins and fens

**RANGE** Throughout

**FLOWERS** June–August

**SIMILAR SPECIES** Marsh Valerian, *Valeriana dioica*, smaller, with long **runners** and lobed stem leaves. Flowers pink. Fens, marshes and bogs. March–June.

An escape from gardens now very widely spread in the wild. A beautiful plant, with opposite, rather shiny, oval, pointed leaves and clusters of red, sometimes pink or white, flowers. Each flower is 8–10 mm long. Very attractive to butterflies, bees and other insects.

**SIZE** To 80 cm

**HABITAT** Gardens, walls, cliffs, railway embankments

**RANGE** Scattered, commonest in S and W. Absent from most of Scotland, and in Ireland mainly in S and E.

**FLOWERS** June–August

*Dipsacus fullonum*

A tall, tough-stemmed, prickly plant with oval, spiny **flowerheads**, about 8 cm long. The individual tiny **florets** are purple (sometimes white). Often used in displays of 'everlasting' dried flowers. The seeds, which develop inside the flowerheads, attract birds such as Goldfinches.

**SIZE** To 2 m

**HABITAT** Riverbanks, roadsides, hedges, waste land

**RANGE** Common in England, mainly in S. Absent from much of Scotland and Ireland.

**FLOWERS** July–August

# Field Scabious

*Knautia arvensis*

A handsome plant with rather flat heads of bluish-lilac flowers, each
**flowerhead** about 3–4 cm across. The stems are rough and hairy.
The stem leaves are deeply cut and the base leaves spoon-shaped.

**SIZE** To 1 m

**HABITAT** Dry grassland, banks

**RANGE** Throughout, but rare in N Scotland and NW Ireland

**FLOWERS** July–September

# Small Scabious

*Scabiosa columbaria*

A smaller version of Field Scabious (p.205), with smaller, bluish-violet **flowerheads** about 15–30 mm across. When fruiting, the honeycomb texture of the oval heads is very distinctive. The base leaves are spoon-shaped and the stem leaves **pinnate**.

**SIZE** To 70 cm

**HABITAT** Dry chalk grassland, banks

**RANGE** Throughout England and Wales, but not in Ireland, nor most of Scotland

**FLOWERS** July–August

A rather tall plant with oval leaves at its base and narrow stem-leaves. The flowering heads are rounded and about 20–25 mm across. The flowers are a deeper purple-blue than those of Field Scabious (p.205) and Small Scabious (p.206). Its strange name comes from the short root, which looks as though it has been bitten off. The Devil is supposed to have bitten it off to destroy its medicinal properties.

**SIZE** To 1 m

**HABITAT** Marshes, fens, damp meadows and wet woodland

**RANGE** Throughout

**FLOWERS** June–October

One of our most familiar wild flowers, adorning many a lawn, and common everywhere. The bright 'flowers', like those of all composites, are actually made up of a collection of tiny individual flowers (**florets**). The centre of the 'flower' is yellow and is surrounded by white 'petals' (**ray florets**). The leaves are rounded and grow in **rosettes**.

**SIZE** To 12 cm

**HABITAT** Short grassland, lawns, waste ground

**RANGE** Throughout

**FLOWERS** January–December

A familiar species, with feathery leaves and flat clusters of white or pinkish **flowerheads**. Each flowerhead is about 4–6 mm across. Achilles, the hero of Greek legend, is supposed to have used this plant to heal battle wounds in his troops, hence the Latin name. Herbal medicine uses Yarrow for a host of remedies, from healing wounds, to remedies for colds and fever, stomach ulcers and rheumatism.

**SIZE** To 60 cm

**HABITAT** Grassland, waste land, hedges, roadsides, lawns

**RANGE** Throughout

**FLOWERS** June–August

# Pineappleweed

*Matricaria matricarioides*

A strong smell of pineapple distinguishes this somewhat scruffy looking plant. It has rather odd-looking **flowerheads** which lack the spreading, petal-like **florets** of most members of the daisy family (see Daisy, p.208). Its leaves are finely divided, with narrow, pointed lobes. It was introduced from America in 1871, and has now spread everywhere.

**SIZE** To 30 cm

**HABITAT** Footpaths, waste ground, roadsides, bridleways and cart tracks

**RANGE** Throughout

**FLOWERS** May–August

# Scentless Mayweed

*Tripleurospermum inodorum*

The commonest daisy-like weed of arable fields and waste ground. As its name suggests, it has no obvious scent. The daisy-like (p.208) **flowerheads** are large (to 4.5 cm across), with a flattish centre. The leaves are deeply dissected.

**SIZE** To 60 cm

**HABITAT** A weed of arable fields, waste ground, footpath edges and sea shores

**RANGE** Throughout

**FLOWERS** July–September

**SIMILAR SPECIES** Scented Mayflower, *Matricaria recutita*; domed flowers; common aromatic arable weed.

Like Scentless Mayweed (p.211), this species has large (2–3 cm across), daisy-like **flowerheads** (see p.208), but is pleasantly scented. The plant is hairy and the leaves are often woolly underneath.

**SIZE** To 50 cm

**HABITAT** Arable land and waste ground, on lime-rich soils

**RANGE** Mainly in S and E England, scattered in E Scotland

**FLOWERS** June–July

**SIMILAR SPECIES** Stinking Chamomile, *Anthemis cotula*, related, similar, but smells unpleasant and is hairless. Arable fields on heavy soils. S and E England, July–September.

A large-flowered daisy-like plant (p.208), with flowering heads held high on long stalks. The **flowerheads** can be as large as 6 cm across. The base leaves are spoon-shaped and about 10 cm long. The stem leaves are more oblong and toothed. Also called Marguerite or Moon-daisy. An even larger form, known by the same names, is often grown in gardens and also turns up in the wild.

**SIZE** To 70 cm

**HABITAT** Grassland

**RANGE** Throughout

**FLOWERS** June–August

*Tanacetum vulgare*

A stiff plant with deep green leaves and dark, purplish stems. The yellow **flowerheads** are tight and button-like (about 7–12 mm across), and grow in loose clusters. Tansy contains a natural insecticide – the leaves used to be strewn on floors to deter fleas. Also used in herbal medicines to treat infection by threadworms.

**SIZE** To 1.2 m

**HABITAT** Waste ground, hedges, roadsides

**RANGE** Throughout, but scattered in Ireland

**FLOWERS** July–September

Very aromatic, with a characteristic musky smell. The leaves are a light yellow-green. The **flowerheads** each look rather like a Daisy (p.208), with a yellow centre surrounded by a ring of short 'petals' (actually special flowers or **ray florets**). As you would expect from its name, Feverfew is an effective medicinal herb. It has been proved to help relieve migraine and other headaches, as well as arthritis and asthma.

**SIZE** To 60 cm

**HABITAT** Waste ground, walls, old gardens, hedges, roadsides

**RANGE** Throughout, but rather scattered in N and W Scotland and in Ireland

**FLOWERS** July–August

# Mugwort

216 *Artemisia vulgaris*

A very common roadside plant with tall, bushy growth, reddish stems and divided leaves. The **flowerheads** are very small (2–3 mm across), red-brown and inconspicuous, and are wind-pollinated. Mugwort was thought to have magic properties and was used to ward off evil spirits.

**SIZE** To 1.2 m

**HABITAT** Waste land, roadsides, banks, hedges

**RANGE** Throughout, but mainly coastal in Scotland

**FLOWERS** July–September

A tall, bushy plant with fluffy, pinkish clusters of **flowerheads** (each 2–5 mm across) which attract many insects, including butterflies. The leaves are toothed, divided and arranged opposite each other on the stems.

**SIZE** To 1.5 m

**HABITAT** Stream sides, river banks, marshes, fens; also in damp woods

**RANGE** Throughout lowlands, but mainly coastal in Scotland

**FLOWERS** July–September

# Goldenrod

218 *Solidago virgaurea*

Goldenrod has tall flowering stems with **spikes** of yellow-gold
**flowerheads**. Each flowerhead is about 10 mm across, with 6–12
rays. The base leaves are spoon-shaped and stalked, the stem leaves
**lanceolate** and unstalked. This species is used in herbal medicine to
treat urinary infection, arthritis, catarrh and diarrhoea.

**SIZE** To 75 cm

**HABITAT** Dry woods, grassland, rocks, cliffs, hedges, dunes

**RANGE** Throughout, although rarer in E and central England, and
central Ireland

**FLOWERS** July–September

**SIMILAR SPECIES** The larger Canadian Goldenrod, *Solidago
canadensis,* often escapes from gardens to wasteland.

A late-flowering plant with yellow **flowerheads** to about 3 cm across, and broad, pointed leaves. This plant was burned and its smoke used to drive away fleas, hence the name.

**SIZE** To 60 cm

**HABITAT** Marshes, wet meadows, ditches

**RANGE** Throughout England, Wales and S Ireland; rarer in N and absent from most of Scotland.

**FLOWERS** August–September

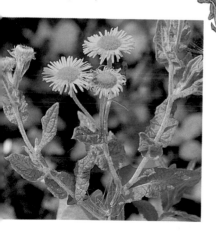

# Butterbur

*Petasites hybridus*

This plant has large leaves (a bit like rhubarb leaves), and is commonly seen along stream banks. The flowers, which appear before the leaves, are purplish-pink and arranged in very solid **spikes**. Each flower is 3–12 mm across. The male and female plants are separate, and female plants are rare in parts of lowland England. The leaves were once used to wrap butter, hence the common name.

**SIZE** To 80 cm

**HABITAT** Wet meadows by streams, often under trees

**RANGE** Throughout, but rarer in central and N Scotland.

**FLOWERS** March–May

Like Butterbur (p.220), the flowers of Coltsfoot appear before the leaves. The **flowerheads**, which are 15–35 mm across, are rather like those of Dandelion (p.234), but bend over as they mature. The seeds are also fluffy and windborne. The leaves are triangular, with a heart-shaped base. Coltsfoot has long been used as a herbal medicine for coughs and colds.

**SIZE** To 30 cm

**HABITAT** Waste land, arable fields, roadsides, river banks, dunes, shingle and scree

**RANGE** Throughout

**FLOWERS** March–April

# Ragwort

**DAISY FAMILY**

*Senecio jacobaea*

A tall, yellow-flowered plant, with rather feathery leaves. The flowering heads are arranged in a flat-topped group. Often attacked by the black and yellow caterpillars of the Cinnabar Moth, which may even kill the plant if sufficiently numerous. A serious weed of pastureland, somewhat poisonous to cattle, and also to rabbits which avoid it.

**SIZE** To 1.5 m

**HABITAT** Pastures, waste ground, sand dunes

**RANGE** Throughout

**FLOWERS** June–October

Introduced from Italy, first recorded on old walls in Oxford in 1794, and now a widespread weed. This ragwort has a bushy growth. The leaves are deeply lobed, with narrow leaflets. The **flowerheads** are bright yellow and 15 25 mm across.

**SIZE** To 40 cm

**HABITAT** Old walls, waste ground, especially by railways

**RANGE** Throughout England and Wales; rare in Ireland and Scotland

**FLOWERS** June–December

This common garden weed differs from the other ragworts (pp.222, 223) in not having any obvious **ray florets**. The yellow **flowerheads** are cylindrical, not flat like those of the Daisy (p.208), and about 4 mm across. The leaves are shiny above, with rather blunt lobes. It is a rather weak plant with succulent stems.

**SIZE** To 45 cm

**HABITAT** Waste ground, arable fields, gardens

**RANGE** Throughout

**FLOWERS** January–December

Burdocks are robust, bushy plants with large leaves and characteristic hooked fruits, or burs, which cling to animal fur or to clothing. There are several species, but they are difficult to distinguish, although the burdocks themselves are easy to recognize as a group. The large leaves are rough and heart-shaped. The **flowerheads** are rounded and develop the hooked spines when in fruit. The plant is used to add a bitter flavour to drinks (e.g. dandelion and burdock) and also in herbal medicine to treat skin disorders.

**SIZE** To 2.5 m

**HABITAT** Waste places, roadsides, open woods

**RANGE** Throughout

**FLOWERS** July–September

**SIMILAR SPECIES** Greater Burdock, *Arctium lappa*

# Musk Thistle

*Carduus nutans*

One of the prettiest thistles, with nodding purple heads of sweet-smelling flowers, the heads are 4–6 cm across. The leaves are lobed and tipped with sharp spines. The stems have spiny wings which stop well below the **flowerheads**. Beloved of bees, butterflies and other nectar feeding insects.

**SIZE** To 1 m

**HABITAT** Waste places, arable fields, roadsides and rough pastures

**RANGE** Mainly in England, Wales and SE Scotland, but not in Ireland

**FLOWERS** May–August

**SIMILAR SPECIES** Welted Thistle, *Carduus acanthoides*, stem winged to flowerheads. Grass verges, waste land, stream banks. Common in S; rare Ireland. June–August.

Also known as Field Thistle, this is a very common weed of fields and pastures. The dull purple flowering heads are small (to 2.5 cm) and clustered. Like most thistles, it is well protected by prickly leaves, which have triangular lobes. The stem is not winged. The plant spreads by creeping through the soil.

**SIZE** To 1 m

**HABITAT** Fields, pastures, waste ground

**RANGE** Throughout

**FLOWERS** July–September

**SIMILAR SPECIES** Spear Thistle, *Cirsium vulgare*, similar but stem spiny and winged, red-purple **flowerheads** larger. Fields, pastures, waste ground, gardens throughout. July–October.

Like the Spear Thistle (p.227), this species has a spiny winged stem, but is usually taller and has smaller **flowerheads** (usually less than 2 cm across). These are dark reddish purple (rarely white). The leaves are deeply divided and spiny.

**SIZE** To 2 m

**HABITAT** Marsh, wet grassland, wet woods

**RANGE** Throughout

**FLOWERS** July–September

# Common Knapweed

A hairy plant with tough, grooved stems and mostly undivided leaves. The **flowerheads** are tightly-packed, red-purple and about 2–4 cm across, opening from rather hard buds.

**SIZE** To 65 cm

**HABITAT** Grassland, roadsides, hedges, cliffs

**RANGE** Throughout

**FLOWERS** June–September

**SIMILAR SPECIES** Greater Knapweed, *Centaurea scabiosa*, divided leaves and larger, decorative flowerheads. Similar habitats throughout lowlands, common in S and Ireland. July–September.

A tall, slender plant with grass-like leaves and large yellow **flowerheads** (to 5 cm across) which open only in the morning sun. This gives rise to the alternative name of Jack-go-to-bed-at-noon. The flowers develop into hairy fruiting heads like giant dandelion clocks, hence their common name.

**SIZE** To 70 cm

**HABITAT** Grassland, roadsides, waste ground, dunes

**RANGE** Throughout England, but less common in W and in Wales. Scattered in Scotland and Ireland.

**FLOWERS** June–July

# Smooth Sow-thistle

This common plant has hairless leaves without spines (unlike most sow-thistles), and pale yellow **flowerheads**, each about 2.5 cm across. Like the other sow-thistles it has milky juice in the stem and leaves.

**SIZE** To 1.5 m

**HABITAT** Waste land, cultivated ground

**RANGE** Throughout, except Scottish highlands

**FLOWERS** June–August

**SIMILAR SPECIES** Prickly Sow-thistle, *Sonchus asper*, spiny leaves and similar sized flowerheads. Throughout, June–August.

# Field Sow-thistle

*Sonchus arvensis*

A tall, creeping plant with large yellow **flowerheads**, 4–5 cm across. The leaves have spiny, toothed edges. The upper parts of the stems often have a covering of yellowish hair. Like other sow-thistles, it has milky juice in the stem and leaves.

**SIZE** To 1.5 m

**HABITAT** Stream sides, banks, roadsides, drift-lines of the sea and of rivers

**RANGE** Throughout, but mainly coastal in Scotland

**FLOWERS** July–October

Wiry stems and many small, yellow **flowerheads** (10–15 mm across) characterize this common species. The leaves are lobed, with a triangular lobe at the end. The fruits ripen inside small conical heads.

**SIZE** To 75 cm; often smaller

**HABITAT** Grassland, heath, walls, roadsides, waste ground

**RANGE** Throughout

**FLOWERS** June–September

**SIMILAR SPECIES** Rough Hawk's-beard, *Crepis biennis*

One of our most familiar flowers, with **rosettes** of long, backwardly-toothed leaves, and large yellow **flowerheads** on smooth, hollow, leafless stalks. Dandelion leaves, favourite food of pet rabbits and guinea pigs, may also be added to salads to add an extra, rather bitter flavour. The plant is also used to treat skin diseases and rheumatism.

**SIZE** To 30 cm

**HABITAT** Roadsides, waste ground, lawns

**RANGE** Throughout

**FLOWERS** March–October

Like a tall Dandelion (p.234), with branched, leafless
stems and flat yellow **flowerheads** (2.5–4 cm
across). The hairy, oval leaves, which grow in a
**rosette** at the base of the plant, give this
species its common name – they have the
texture and rough shape of a cat's ear.

**SIZE** To 50 cm

**HABITAT** Meadows, pastures, roadsides, dunes

**RANGE** Throughout

**FLOWERS** June–September

Very similar to Cat's Ear (p.235), but its yellow **flowerheads** are usually reddish underneath and smaller, 12–35 mm across. These grow on leafless, branched, slender stems. The leaves are deeply lobed, pointed and not obviously hairy, unlike those of Cat's Ear. They grow as a **rosette** at ground level.

**SIZE** To 50 cm

**HABITAT** Meadows, pastures, waste ground, screes, rocks

**RANGE** Throughout

**FLOWERS** June–October

**SIMILAR SPECIES** Rough Hawkbit, *Leontodon hispidus*, hairy, unbranched stems, large golden flowerheads. Chalk grassland, England, Wales, S Scotland, central Ireland. June–September

Most common hawkweeds have leafy stems and several **flowerheads**, usually light yellow and 1–4 cm across (depending on the species). There are many species, but most are difficult to identify, although they are easy to recognize as a group. Some are common on roadsides and railway banks, and generally flower in mid to late summer. The photograph shows *Hieracium vulgatum*, probably the most common hawkweed in N England and Scotland.

**SIZE** To 1 m

**HABITAT** Roadsides, grassland, rocky places

**RANGE** The group is widespread. *Hieracium vulgatum* is common in in N England and Scotland; N Ireland.

**FLOWERS** May–August

# Mouse-ear Hawkweed

**DAISY FAMILY**

*Hieracium pilosella*

Unlike many hawkweeds which are all confusingly similar, this common species is easy to identify. It is rather low-growing, with long, white **runners** and **rosettes** of thick leaves with white felty hairs underneath. It is these leaves which give the plant its common name. The single **flowerheads** are yellow, with red streaks beneath, and 15–25 mm across.

**SIZE** To 25 cm

**HABITAT** Grassland, heaths, walls, banks

**RANGE** Throughout

**FLOWERS** May–August

**DAISY FAMILY**

# Bristly Oxtongue

*Picris echioides*  239

A tall plant with prickly hairs on its wavy-edged, pimply leaves, and large yellow **flowerheads** 20–25 mm across. Below each flowerhead there are five heart-shaped **bracts**.

**SIZE** To 1 m

**HABITAT** Waste ground, roadsides, hedges, field margins, especially on heavy, chalky soils

**RANGE** Mainly lowland England and Wales; rare in Scotland and Ireland

**FLOWERS** June–October

**SIMILAR SPECIES** Hawkweed Oxtongue, *Picris hieracioides*, lacks pimples, and bracts smaller. Lowland England and Wales; rare Scotland and Ireland. July–September.

# Lily-of-the-valley

**LILY FAMILY**

*Convallaria majalis*

A pretty garden plant, which also grows wild in some places. It has long oval leaves, with flowering stems growing up in between. The bell-shaped, white flowers (each about 8 mm long) are sweetly scented and arranged in a loose, drooping cluster. Extracts of this plant are used in medicine to regulate the heart beat.

**SIZE** To 20 cm

**HABITAT** Native in dry limestone woods; sometimes naturalized from gardens.

**RANGE** Scattered in England and E Wales; rare in Scotland; rare in Ireland (introduced).

**FLOWERS** May–June

The broad, pointed leaves smell of onion when crushed, and often carpet the ground. The white clusters of star-shaped flowers, each to 2 cm across, appear in the spring. The leaves have a pleasant mild garlic flavour, hence it is also known as Wild Garlic.

**SIZE** To 45 cm

**HABITAT** Damp woods, shady copses

**RANGE** Throughout, but rare in NE Scotland, and much of S and W Ireland

**FLOWERS** April–June

# Bluebell

*Hyacinthoides non-scripta*

One of our most attractive wild flowers which tends to grow in large patches on the woodland floor. A Bluebell wood in May can be an unforgettable sight. The leaves are long and narrow. The flowers are bright blue (rarely white or pink) and bell-shaped and grow clustered together in groups of 4–16. The flowers are each about 2 cm long.

**SIZE** To 50 cm

**HABITAT** Woods, hedges, banks

**RANGE** Throughout, but more scattered in S Ireland

**FLOWERS** April–June

**SIMILAR SPECIES** Garden Bluebells are usually *Hyacinthoides hispanica*, or hybrids of *H. hispanica* and *H. non-scripta*.

A small coastal plant with narrow, shiny, twisted leaves. The flowers are pale violet-blue and grow in clusters of 2–12 on each stem. Each flower measures about 10 mm across. The flowers face upwards and open widely, unlike those of the Bluebell (p.242).

**SIZE** To 15 cm

**HABITAT** Grassland near the coast, cliff tops

**RANGE** Mainly along N and W coasts; also on parts of E coast in Scotland and N England; and E coast of Ireland.

**FLOWERS** April–May

244 *Narcissus pseudonarcissus*

The true Wild Daffodil is small by the standards of many garden varieties, but is still large for a wildflower. It also tends to grow in groups, so can be an impressive sight. The flowers are pale yellow, with a deep yellow trumpet-like tube, and up to 6 cm long. The leaves are grey-green, long, thin and flattened.

**SIZE** To 35 cm

**HABITAT** Damp woods and grassland

**RANGE** Commonest in the W of England; introduced to some parts of Scotland and Ireland.

**FLOWERS** March–April

# Snowdrop

*Galanthus nivalis* 245

A very familiar winter-flowering plant with white
nodding flowers (one flower to each flower-stalk),
each about 2.5 cm long . The leaves are grey-
green and long and narrow. This is another
species which is often planted in gardens, and
also often escapes into the wild. It may be native
to parts of W England and Wales.

**SIZE** To 20 cm

**HABITAT** Damp woods, stream banks

**RANGE** Scattered throughout Britain; rare in Ireland.

**FLOWERS** January–March

# Yellow Iris

*Iris pseudacorus*

Also called Yellow Flag, this familiar tall plant has long,
flattened leaves and large, bright yellow flowers, each
up to 10 cm across, with 2–3 flowers on each stem. It
grows from a thick **rhizome** at the base. There are
many garden varieties of iris, with large flowers in
many colours.

**SIZE** To 1.5 m

**HABITAT** Marshes, ponds, riversides, wet woods

**RANGE** Throughout

**FLOWERS** May–July

**SIMILAR SPECIES** Stinking Iris, *Iris foetidissima*, similar
leaves, but an unpleasant smell. Flowers smaller, dull purple. Woods,
hedges, sea cliffs, mainly S England and Wales, May–July.

A small, pretty orchid with flowers that look rather like bumble bees, each about 2 cm across. In some parts of its range, though not in Britain, it is pollinated by bumblebees, which are fooled by the flower into trying to mate with what looks like another bee. The base leaves are oval and blunt, the stem-leaves rather pointed.

**SIZE** To 45 cm

**HABITAT** Pastures, banks, chalk grassland

**RANGE** Scattered in England, Wales and Ireland

**FLOWERS** June–July

# Early Purple Orchid

248 *Orchis mascula*

A common orchid, with glossy green, black-spotted leaves and purple flowers. The flowers grow together in a loose **spike** sticking up from the centre of a **rosette** of base leaves. Each flower is about 8–12 mm across. One of the earliest orchids to come into flower.

**SIZE** To 60 cm

**HABITAT** Woods and open pastures

**RANGE** Throughout

**FLOWERS** April–June

# Marsh Orchids

The marsh orchids are a difficult group to identify; there are several rather similar species, and hybrids with intermediate features also occur. They have pink or purple flowers, each marked by darker dots and lines, and each about 10 mm across. Unlike those of the Early Purple Orchid (p.248), the base leaves do not grow in a **rosette**, and they may be spotted or unspotted depending on the species. The species illustrated here is Southern Marsh Orchid *Dactylorhiza praetermissa*.

**SIZE** To 60 cm

**HABITAT** Wet meadows, marshes, fens, wet dunes

**RANGE** Scattered throughout

**FLOWERS** May–August

*Dactylorhiza fuchsii*

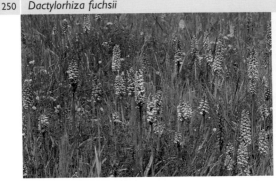

The flowers of this orchid are pale pink with darker spots or streaks, and grow in a cylindrical **spike**. Each flower is about 15 mm across. It has several broad, rather blunt-ended leaves, each marked with broad dark spots.

**SIZE** To 60 cm

**HABITAT** Woods, marshes, meadows

**RANGE** Throughout, except Scottish Highlands

**FLOWERS** June–August

**SIMILAR SPECIES** Heath Spotted Orchid, *Dactylorhiza maculata*, similar but pyramidal spike, whitish to pale purple flowers and round spots on leaves. Woods or acid soils throughout, rare in E England. June–August.

# Common Twayblade

*Listera ovata*

It is often hard to spot this orchid because it has inconspicuous yellow-green flowers which do not stand out against other plants. The flowers grow in a **spike** up to 25 cm tall. Best told by the twin (or tway) rounded leaves towards the base of the single stem.

**SIZE** To 60 cm

**HABITAT** Wet woods, pastures, dunes

**RANGE** Throughout, but rather rare inland in central and N Scotland

**FLOWERS** June–July

**SIMILAR SPECIES** Lesser Twayblade, *Listera cordata*, shorter, with smaller leaves. Mountain woods and moorland, mainly in Scotland. July–September.

252 *Arum maculatum*

The shiny arrow-shaped leaves grow in the spring, to be followed by strange hooded flowers. Each 'flower' is a central purple rod (the **spadix**) enclosed by a translucent hood (the **spathe**). The spathe is up to 25 cm tall. It is the **spadix** which carries the tiny separate male and female flowers. The **flowerheads** have an unpleasant smell which attracts flies for pollination. Clusters of poisonous red berries develop later.

**SIZE** To 50 cm

**HABITAT** Woods, hedges, banks

**RANGE** Throughout, except central and N Scotland

**FLOWERS** April–May

# Index